44 Ways to Expand the Teaching Ministry of Your Church

LYLE E.
Schaller

44 Ways to Expand the Teaching Ministry of Your Church

ABINGDON PRESS / Nashville

44 WAYS TO EXPAND THE TEACHING MINISTRY OF YOUR CHURCH

Library of Congress Cataloging-in-Publication Data

SCHALLER, LYLE E.
    44 ways to expand the teaching ministry of your church /
Lyle E. Schaller.
        p. cm.
    Includes bibliographical references.
    ISBN 0-687-13289-4 (alk. paper)
    1. Christian education. I. Title. II. Title: Forty-four ways
to expand the teaching ministry of your church.
BV1471.2.S26 1992
268'. 1--dc20   91-14234
                                                        CIP

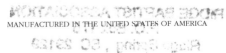

MANUFACTURED IN THE UNITED STATES OF AMERICA

CONTENTS

INTRODUCTION

Why should anyone be especially interested in expanding the teaching ministry of his or her church when nearly everyone agrees that the central focus should be on preaching and worship, when the most obvious pressing problem is the current financial crisis, and when many critics agree that the Sunday school is an anachronism carried over from the nineteenth century?

One answer begins with viewing every congregation as a passing parade. Every year several people drop out of that parade for one or more reasons. A few die. Others move away. A couple are disenchanted with the new pastor. A husband drops out following the death of his wife. One or two marry into another parish. In the smaller congregations those annual losses usually are equivalent to 3 to 5 percent of the reported membership. In larger churches the annual losses rise to 6 to 9 percent, and in the very large and rapidly growing churches, the turnover rate often runs between 10 and 25 percent year after year.

The teaching ministry often ranks second only to excellent preaching as a means of attracting new people to join that passing parade.

A second response is based on the assumption that, as the decades roll by, what once began as an exciting, attractive, and high-commitment new mission often evolves into a low commitment church. If fewer than one-half of your resident confirmed members are present for the corporate

9

worship of God on the average weekend, that probably means this is a low-commitment congregation. (Many observers will argue that if the proportion of resident members present for worship on the typical weekend is below 70 percent, that is a low-commitment church.)

A useful beginning point in a strategy to move from a low-commitment church is to expand the teaching ministry.

A third response is found in the date. This last decade of the twentieth century has presented most Protestant congregations with two choices. The highly visible choice is to welcome the generations born after 1955 and grow younger and larger. An expansion of the teaching ministry can be the most effective means of reaching, attracting, and serving new generations of younger members. The easier and more widely chosen alternative is to grow smaller in size as the members grow older together.

A fourth reason for expanding the teaching ministry is that it often is the easiest, least divisive, and least costly way to increase the range of choices offered to people who come from several generations and who represent a broad range of values, needs, and desires.

Fifth, as is pointed out repeatedly in this book, an expansion of the teaching ministry can be an effective means of reinforcing the ministry of Word and Sacrament.

Sixth, expanding the teaching ministry can be a highly effective strategy for activating the passive congregation— and this leads to an explanation of the outline.

The most critical issue in expanding your teaching ministry is not techniques. The crucial variable is desire. Thus this book begins with a chapter on priorities. The key to expanding the teaching ministry is to make it the top priority! The second step is to agree on criteria for self-evaluation. A third is the unreserved support of the pastor. In many churches the congregational culture and/or polity are major barriers. Thus the first four chapters discuss these beginning points. The remaining eleven chapters focus on other policy questions, techniques, and fringe benefits.

Finally, two questions merit answers. The first is the request to point out how the contents fulfill the promise of the title. The answer is chapters 1, 2, 3, 4, 6, 7, 8, 10, 11, 12, 13, and 14, each suggesting one way to expand your teaching ministry. Those twelve plus the two on entry points and assimilation in the last chapter add up to fourteen. Add in the fifteen each in chapters 5 and 9 and the grand total is 44. Okay? If your count comes out with 45 or 53 or 71 or 117, be grateful. If it comes out at 37 or 43, please do not sue us!

The second and far more frequently asked question is "Why 44? Why not 42 or 47 or 45?"

Back in 1950 the Minneapolis Lakers defeated the Fort Wayne Pistons in a professional basketball game by a score of 19-18. The reaction to these and other low-scoring games was that a low score took excitement out of the game. The result was the adoption of the 24-second clock rule, which required the team with the ball to shoot for a basket within 24 seconds after gaining possession. Who decided on 24 seconds and why? Coach Biasone decided that in a truly competitive game, the two teams would take twice as many shots as they had been taking. In the typical game of that era the two teams were taking approximately 60 shots a game. Double that and divide 120 into 48 minutes, and the result came out 24 seconds. If Biasone had concluded that 100 shots made for a lively game, the result would have been a 29-second shot clock. If he had chosen 140, the result would have been a 20-second clock.

The moral is that you pick a number that sounds about right and that sets the pattern for years to come. A corollary is what you do today to expand the teaching ministry of your church will carry implications that will be felt a decade later.

CHAPTER ONE

What Are Your Priorities?

First of all, we're looking for a minister who likes people. We want someone who really enjoys being a pastor to people," explained a member of the search committee at the two-hundred-member Forest Park Church. "Number two on our list of qualifications is preaching, and number three is evangelism. We would like to reverse our numerical decline of the past several years and attract more younger folks."

"You're asking what I do best as a pastor?" responded the newly arrived senior minister of the eight-hundred-member congregation. "That's easy. I believe my number-one skill is preaching, number two is administration, and number three is working with people."

"We've come up with six priorities for the next five years," reported the person chairing the Long-Range Planning Committee at Trinity Church. "The first, which I believe everyone here will agree with, is that we need a new roof and we need to tuckpoint the masonry. That is estimated at $5,000. Second, instead of providing a church-owned house, we are recommending paying our minister a housing allowance, razing that old parsonage next door, and paving the land for additional parking. Third, we are recommending that we look for a part-time, semi-retired minister to call in the hospital, visit our shut-ins and elderly members, and preach five or six Sundays a year. Fourth, we believe the time has come to stop relying completely on volunteers to staff our youth

13

program and to hire a part-time college student to carry that responsibility. Fifth, we are recommending that we increase the proportion of our total receipts that are allocated to missions by one percentage point annually. Last year we gave 12 percent to missions, and we believe we should get that up to 17 percent in five years. Finally, we are recommending that we seek a stewardship consultant who can help us raise the level of member giving by at least 25 percent."

———

"What do we do best as a congregation?" reflected a fifty-three-year-old, long-time member during an interview with a parish consultant. "Well, first of all, we're a friendly church. Everybody here loves one another. Second, we take good care of our property. This is a beautiful building. A lot of outsiders ask if they can be married here. We love this church. Third, we enjoy eating together. I guess that's one reason we get along so well. We're an eating church."

———

"When our nominating committee meets, our first job is to identify who will be recommended to be elected as elders," explained a long-time leader in a five-hundred-member congregation. "The session plays a very important role here, and we usually have one or two vacancies every year. Next, we try to fill any vacancies among the deacons. Of course, if any one of the key positions, such as church treasurer, is going to become vacant, we try to fill that first."

———

"When it comes to making appointments, there are two numbers I look at very carefully," explained a United Methodist District Superintendent. "The first is salary and the second is the average attendance at worship."

———

"If you want to attract the church shoppers of today, you need five assets," declared a denominational staff member. "The first is a highly visible and easy-to-find location. The second is an abundance of offstreet parking. The third is excellent preaching, the fourth is superb music, and the fifth is a team of volunteers who will go out and call on your first-time visitors before the sun sets that Sunday."

"If you want to reach the young families of today, you have to offer what they want," explained the person chairing the Christian education committee at Central Church. "The mother and father both work, they're busy, they want life to be convenient, and they don't have the time to spend all Sunday morning at church. I'm telling you, if we are serious about reaching these young families, we need to offer Sunday school and worship at the same hour! The parents can put the kids in Sunday school while they come to church. They want a convenience package, and if we don't offer it, a church down the street will. The real issue is not the schedule. The real issue is do you want to attract today's young families?

Do these comments carry a familiar ring? Do they reflect the world in which you live? Do they describe contemporary reality?

ONE ANSWER FOR THREE QUESTIONS

If they do describe contemporary reality, you have the answer to three questions.

1. Why has the attendance in Sunday school dropped so sharply in recent decades?
Between 1960 and 1990 the population of the United States increased by approximately 40 percent, but Sunday school attendance in at least a dozen denominations dropped by 40 to 50 percent.

15

2. Why are some newer congregations attracting so many of the people born after World War II while most long-established churches find themselves growing older in terms of the median age of the members and smaller in numbers?

3. What is the first step to be taken by the congregation that wants to expand its teaching ministry?

One answer applies to all three questions. The decline in Sunday school is primarily a result of making it a lower priority. Other concerns have moved up past it on the scale of priorities. None of the comments quoted in the beginning of this chapter reflect a high priority for the Sunday school.

Hundreds of newer Protestant congregations have discovered the most effective method for attracting the generations born after 1945 has been to offer attractive, highly structured, carefully designed, and meaningful learning opportunities for both adults and children. The teaching ministry is the road to follow if a major goal is to grow younger and larger.

While it is out on the fringe of this discussion, most of these comments are frequently heard in low-commitment churches. The most obvious example was expressed by the person chairing the Christian education committee at Central Church who advocated the one-hour convenience package. That appeal usually is offered by a low-commitment congregation seeking to reach low-commitment people. The best teaching ministries usually are found in high-commitment churches.

Finally, making the teaching ministry the number-one priority in program planning, in the allocation of scarce resources, and in designing tomorrow is the first and most important step to take in expanding that ministry in your congregation.

That may be difficult, it may be painful, and it proba-bly will not win immediate universal acclaim. How to do that is the theme of this book as we look at forty-three other ways to expand the teaching ministry of your church.

CHAPTER TWO

What Are Your Criteria?

The Sunday morning schedule at Central Church begins with a fifty-minute worship service at eight-thirty, followed by Sunday school at nine-thirty and worship at eleven o'clock.

Shortly before nine on a typical Sunday morning a married couple in their early sixties arrive and go directly to the first-floor room where the Jerusalem Class has been meeting for the past twenty-seven years. The husband immediately begins to prepare the coffee in two thirty-cup coffee makers. One is decaffeinated and the other is regular. While he does this, his wife spreads a cloth over a table and neatly arranges in rows the three choices of pastries she had prepared the night before.

At a quarter after nine a widowed man arrives and inquires if the coffee is ready. "It'll be ready in just a couple of minutes," comes the reply. It is readily apparent, however, that this lonely early arrival is more interested in fellowship and conversation than coffee. By nine-thirty all the regulars have arrived and are busily engaged in small talk, fellowship, mid-morning refreshments, and getting reacquainted with dear friends, some of whom they had not seen for three to six days.

At nine thirty-five the current president of the class begins a largely ignored effort to assemble the class in their chairs. After several minutes of limited success, he asks the volunteer pianist to begin to play "Amazing Grace." Within seconds nearly everyone joins in singing this familiar hymn and by the conclusion most are seated in their places. Several carry their coffee cups to their chairs and finish their coffee after the conclusion of that opening hymn.

The president leads the class in an opening prayer that includes intercessions by name for the two longtime members who are in the hospital, for the widow who just received the news that she has to undergo major surgery within a few days, and for the teenage grandson of a couple who also were longtime members of the class. The grandson had been severely injured in an automobile accident the previous Friday evening.

This prayer is followed by a two-minute report from the class treasurer, who points out that after the quarterly payment he has just made toward the support of a missionary couple in Africa, the balance in the treasury is down to $171.53, and two obligations of $100 each, both for local outreach ministries, are due at the end of this month.

When the president reads the names of the two members with birthdays this week, the class responds with great enthusiasm by singing "Happy Birthday" to the two honorees. This is followed by two oral announcements by the leader. As he concludes his announcements, one member adds, "We just received this postcard from Everett and Hazel, and I'll pass it around for you to read." Everett and Hazel are longtime members who are enjoying a two-week fishing trip in northern Wisconsin.

"Well, I guess we're ready now to turn it over to you, Herb, for today's lesson," announces the class leader as he turns to Herb Adams, who is teaching a six-week unit on the book of Amos.

"Hold it," interrupts Sam Elliott. "When we made the schedule out for this year, my wife and I agreed to host our Saturday evening social for the second weekend in November. It now turns out we're expecting our first grandchild about that time, and Martha may not be here. She plans to be with our daughter when the baby is due. Bob and Ruth Harrison have agreed to take our turn in November if we'll take their spot in October. We can't do that, however, because I'll be out of town on a ten-day business trip over that weekend." After a few minutes of discussion, Nancy Green agrees to swap January, which was her month to entertain the class, with the Elliotts for October.

While this discussion is going on, Evelyn Brice is trying, with limited success, to explain a sign-up sheet she is passing around on a clipboard. This is an opportunity for all members of the class, if they are interested, to go as a group to a play at a nearby college two weeks from this coming Friday evening. Evelyn pleads with the class that she needs a definite yes or no from everyone today in order to obtain the group discount on the tickets.

"Now that we've got that settled, we can ask Herb to lead us in today's lesson," declares the president.

"Pardon me, but I have an announcement," interrupts Betty Olson. "As some of you know, our missions committee is trying to raise the money to buy two hundred blankets for refugees. If any of you would like to contribute to this needy cause, please see me after class. We're looking for contributions of five or ten or twenty dollars."

(It should be noted that Betty Olson is the most respected member of this class. She has earned that respect by her Christian commitment, by her kind and generous personality, by the hundreds of hours she gives every year as a volunteer in Central Church, by her unreserved loyalty, by being the first to come to the aid of someone in need, by her loving concern for the oppressed and downtrodden, by her humility, and by her sacrificial attitude. When Betty identifies a need, no one questions it.)

"O.K., Herb, it's all yours," declares the president, "and be sure to contribute to the blanket fund."

"I have one very important issue that we have to deal

with right now," interrupts Shirley Baxter. "I think all of you know that one of our most loyal members, Anna McGuire, will be getting out of the hospital tomorrow morning. Her daughter had planned to drive over here from Syracuse and take care of her for a few days, but this morning the daughter called me and said that because of some family problems, she won't be able to get here until late Monday afternoon. As you know, I still work, so I can't do it, but we need someone who can pick Anna up at the hospital about ten o'clock tomorrow morning, take her home, and look after her until her daughter arrives."

After at least forty seconds of complete silence, Woody Churchill speaks, "Well, I guess Sally and I can do it. After class, Shirley, can you give us more exact instructions on what we should do and give us the daughter's telephone number?"

As soon as Woody finishes his sentence, Bert Peacock asks, "Does anyone know the date of our pastor's birthday? I believe it's this coming Thursday. If it is, I think our class ought to give him a present, maybe buy him a book."

"We'll appoint you a committee of one to look into that, Bert, and to take the appropriate action," declares the class leader somewhat impatiently, but with a smile. "You are hereby authorized to spend up to twenty dollars out of the class treasury for the appropriate present and to deliver it on behalf of our class."

At five minutes after ten, Herb Adams begins to present the lesson he had prepared on the eighth chapter of Amos. Herb has made a respectable living over the past thirty-five years selling life insurance, he identifies himself as a self-taught Bible scholar, and he enjoys his twice-a-year, six-week tour of duty teaching the Jerusalem Class. While the class averages about thirty-seven or thirty-eight in attendance on a year-around basis, attendance rarely falls below forty-three or forty-four when Herb is the teacher.

When he left home that morning, Herb had been completely unaware of the missions committee's goal to raise the money to purchase two hundred blankets for refugees, but when he heard Betty Olson's announcement, he decided to incorporate her plea into the day's lesson.

"Instead of hoping that a few of us will give Betty five or ten dollars for those blankets, I think our class should accept the challenge and contribute the money to buy all two hundred," challenged Herb.

"That's a good idea!" exclaimed Ruth Harrison. "Why don't we take up a special offering here in our class to buy two hundred blankets?"

After several minutes of discussion, including the objection that the bylaws of this class forbid special financial appeals, it is agreed by common consent that a second offering will be received next Sunday with all the money received to be given to the missions committee for blankets.

The bell announcing the end of the Sunday school hour rings at ten-thirty, but the discussion on this special appeal is so intense that everyone ignores it. About a quarter to eleven, Herb Adams asks the members of the class to join him in a closing prayer. Before that, he announces that next Sunday, which will be his sixth and last Sunday for this series, he will focus on the permanent value of Amos among all the minor prophets.

The attendance in the Jerusalem Class on this Sunday is forty-four. Of those forty-four, nine had attended the first worship service. Four of the other thirty-five were so busy discussing some personal concerns after class that they did not arrive in the nave until eleven-fifteen. Five had quietly slipped out shortly after the bell rang to robe and warm up with the chancel choir. Two of the men spent the rest of the morning in the kitchen drinking coffee and talking. Sally and Woody Churchill cornered Shirley Baxter to discover exactly what was expected of them when they picked up

Anna McGuire at the hospital the following morning. The three of them walked into the nave during the singing of the last verse of the opening hymn. Seventeen of the remaining twenty-one attenders in that class were in their traditional pews by ten-fifty-eight, but six of them might not have made it to worship that Sunday morning without the peer pressure of their friends. Two of the remaining four persons in the Jerusalem Class had attended only a few times since the arrival of the current pastor three years earlier. The other two left Sunday school to drive sixty miles to eat Sunday dinner with their son and new daughter-in-law.

How do you evaluate the Jerusalem Class?

Before answering that question, it may help to review the history of this class. It had been organized forty-four years earlier by the pastor of that era as a class for young, newly married couples. The fifty-one-year-old pastor of that era was something of a father figure to many of these young adults, and he taught that new class about forty-five Sundays annually for the first three years. By then, the sense of cohesion was sufficiently strong that he was able to resign this role and leave to organize another new class. For the past forty-one years the leadership has come out of the membership. Six members each take a six-week period of serving as the teacher while Herb Adams takes two six-week terms. Many years ago the class agreed they would not meet during August. The four officers each serve a two-year term. One is president, another is the vice-president, a third chairs the social committee, and the fourth is the treasurer. The current class budget of $3,200 includes $2,400 toward the partial support of a missionary who had been reared in that congregation, $100 for the church kitchen, $200 toward the transportation costs for the high school youth's summer work camp trip, and $500 for various local and regional outreach ministries. The special appeal for blankets raised an additional $1,065 on that one Sunday.

During these forty-four years the median age of the membership of the Jerusalem Class has climbed from twenty-eight to fifty-seven years. In the typical year approximately two-thirds of the new members of the class are younger than the median age of the current members, and one-third are older.

Six of the original twenty-eight charter members are still in the class, but each is forty-four years older. The current president is the fifty-eight-year-old son of a minister who joined the class seventeen years ago. He is an extroverted, gregarious, compassionate, friendly, good-humored, patient, and well-organized individual who is the sales manager for a local manufacturing firm. The treasurer is a retired barber who has been a respected and loyal member for nearly forty years. The forty-seven-year-old vice-president joined three years ago and is the youngest member of the class. What began as a class for young newlyweds has evolved into a class of middle-aged and retired adults, including seven widows, two widowers, and three women who never married. On the typical Sunday morning the attenders include about fifteen men and two dozen women.

While the members identify themselves as "middle class," by most criteria this is a collection of upper-middle income adults. With only three or four exceptions, the members clearly are financially more comfortable than their parents were at the same age.

The fifty-three people on the membership roll have a combined total of seventy-nine living children. Six of those seventy-nine children have been divorced at least twice and another thirteen have been divorced once. One result is that these people are far more accepting of divorce and remarriage than their parents were at the same age.

Eight members of the class are in their second marriage, and one man has been married, divorced, remarried, widowed, and remarried. Their presence also tempers any harsh judgments about divorce and remarriage.

Five of the couples and one of the widows has a son who is gay or a daughter who is lesbian, and eight of those parents are aware of their child's sexual orientation. Seven of those eight can be counted on to articulate a compassionate-to-sympathetic perspective whenever the subject of homosexuality surfaces in discussions.

Approximately one-third of today's regular attenders currently hold a responsible leadership position, and another third fit into the category of older ex-leaders. (Three of them are angry and alienated older ex-leaders who are convinced that the arrival of the current pastor has turned out to be the most unfortunate event in this congregation's seventy-nine-year history.)

While it was never discussed in these terms, several of those who subsequently became influential congregational leaders first practiced their ecclesiastical leadership skills while serving as officers in the Jerusalem Class.

Most of the members of this adult Sunday school class feel a deeper sense of loyalty to the class than they do to Central Church or to that denomination. The previous pastor had complained that it was "a little church that really is not a part of Central Church." That was far from a misrepresentation of reality. Many of the members are more likely to be absent from Sunday morning worship than to miss any gathering of this closely-knit fellowship.

It is such a cohesive fellowship that every year some of the older new members, who visit for a few Sundays with the expectation of eventually joining, do not return. They conclude it is an exclusionary group that really is not interested in adding new members. By contrast, every year anywhere from two to five newcomers come back Sunday after Sunday and soon become fully assimilated into this fellowship. One of the more astute longtime members commented, "The newcomers who make the effort to come to our Saturday night social gatherings once a month usually continue to come and to become permanent members. Most of those who show up only on Sunday morning soon disappear." He made this observation in the same way that one would comment on the weather. That's how it is, and there is not much you can do to change it.

About fifteen years ago the governing board at Central Church, in the interest of better money management and to take advantage of high interest rates, had decreed that all the many separate funds and treasuries in the church would be consolidated into one bank account with one treasurer, and that all the interest earned would be credited to the church's general fund. Five members of the Jerusalem Class were on the governing board at the time. They all supported that motion, which was adopted by a unanimous vote. It never occurred to anyone in the Jerusalem Class that the motion applied to them. The class continues to have its own treasury, its own bank account, and its own treasurer. All interest earned on that account goes into the class treasury. A few years ago, to avoid any possible confusion or misunderstanding, the class treasurer moved that account to a different bank than the one used by the church treasurer.

How do you evaluate the Jerusalem Class?

If nutrition is one of the criteria for evaluation, this class is a disaster. One-half of the members are overweight, and the last thing they need is to spend fifteen to thirty minutes every Sunday morning stuffing themselves with rich pastries! An argument can be made in favor of a midmorning beverage, but it would be healthier if that were fruit juice or water, not coffee.

If an open and receptive stance toward prospective new members is one of the criteria, this class fails the test. Approximately one-half of the first-time visitors who display a serious interest in becoming members leave feeling unwanted, ignored, or rejected.

If stewardship and the financial support of missions is an

important criterion, this class almost earns a passing grade. That generous response to the appeal for blankets for refugees was a memorable success story, but this group of people easily could contribute $35,000 annually to missions without any negative impact on their contributions to Central Church and other charitable causes. Disciplined sacrificial giving probably would raise that figure to at least $75,000 annually.

If a mission of every class is to save souls, how does the Jerusalem Class rank? When was the last time a non-believer joined this class and one day suddenly experienced that act of salvation of accepting Jesus Christ as Lord and Savior? Perhaps never? This is not an evangelistic class.

If loyal and unreserved support of the pastor is a criterion, this class may deserve a passing grade, but barely so.

If the proclamation and study of God's word is the central criterion for evaluation, this class fails that test. When the time spent in those monthly social events is added to the time spent in pre-class and post-class fellowship plus the time wasted on announcements, a generous estimate is one-eighth of the time is spent in a formal learning setting.

If reaching and assimilating new generations of young adults is a high priority at Central Church, the Jerusalem Class does little to help implement it. This class is primarily for middle-aged or elderly people who enjoy growing old together!

If learning more about the biblical story is the goal, this class also fails to meet that standard. Only Herb Adams and one other of the regular teachers consistently teach the Bible. The other five volunteer teachers usually pick a book for the class to study or choose a self-help topic or show videotapes to fill up their time.

If every class is to be viewed as an integral part of a larger congregation-wide or denominationally structured approach to Christian education, this remarkably independent class ranks at the bottom of that list. Herb Adams made a superb presentation when he concluded that six-week study of Amos with a summary of the permanent value of Amos among the minor prophets. It is doubtful, however, if five of those present could have passed a test six months later on Herb's presentation.

If good stewardship demands an efficient use of time, this class also fails that test.

If every congregation should be organized around the centrality of the corporate worship of God, the Jerusalem Class clearly is a subversive force at Central Church.

If adherence to the policies adopted by the governing board is a test of loyalty, the Jerusalem Class is disloyal. They have ignored the decree ordering a unified financial system as they have ignored dozens of other decrees from the governing board at Central Church. Several years ago the class officers were instructed by the Christian Education Committee at Central Church to begin using one of the adult curriculum series published by the parent denomination. Two of the officers briefly examined a couple of sample quarterlies and rejected that order in favor of giving each volunteer teacher complete control over the topic to be studied.

How do you evaluate the Jerusalem Class?

From this writer's perspective it is an outstanding success story! This class both teaches and acts out the Christian ethic of love. This class acts out the second great commandment of Jesus to love one's neighbor. It does not meet the needs of the majority of the middle-aged and older adults at Central Church, but it is a meaningful support group for those who need and want an intimate, loving, caring, supportive, and faithful fellowship. For those who need a "third place" beyond that place of residence and that place of work,[1] the Jerusalem Class provides an ideal third place.

Several ministers at Central Church have preached stirring

sermons on Isaiah 6:8, but none was more meaningful to that long-time member, Anna McGuire, than when Shirley Baxter asked for someone to pick Anna up at the hospital on a Monday morning, and Woody Churchill replied, "Here I am! Send me."

This class stands out as an effective organization for the assimilation of some, but not all, new members. It has been especially valuable in retaining the loyalty and participation of members who easily could have dropped out of church completely when their feelings were hurt. It has provided a redundant channel to enable people to support worldwide missions beyond the program designed by the missions committee. It has been especially effective in motivating at least a dozen adults to get up in the morning, to come to this class, and to "stay for church"—adults who otherwise might have found it tempting to "skip church today."

For forty years this class has been a valuable component of a larger informal system of identifying, enlisting, training, placing, and supporting volunteer leaders at Central Church.

Perhaps most important of all, this class has served as a loving and supportive community for members experiencing personal hardships, including the death of a loved one, the breakup of a marriage, or the discovery that they have limited influence over their children's lives.

Others may argue the number-one contribution of this class has been to serve as a sympathetic, supportive, challenging, dependable, and non-judgmental community of faith that accompanies each member on his or her personal religious pilgrimage.

A half dozen people in the Jerusalem Class insist that to them its biggest value has been that it was here when they returned after an absence of several years. Four of these members moved to other states for an extended period of time and returned to find a new pastor who did not remember them, a new governing board that had adopted a new set of program goals, and several hundred new members who viewed them as first-time visitors. Only in the Jerusalem Class were they greeted as old friends who had returned to fill what were still vacant spots in that fellowship. The other two had become disenchanted with a pastor, left to go to another church, returned when that pastor left after nine years, and received an unreserved welcome when they came back to the Jerusalem Class. This class offers stability, continuity, predictability, forgiveness, love, and warmth. In the poem "The Death of a Hired Man," Robert Frost wrote, "Home is the place where, when you have to go there, they have to take you in." The Jerusalem Class does this with unreserved love, acceptance, and compassion.

Most long-established congregations resemble that striated rock one sees while driving through a deep cut that was made in the surface of the earth to accommodate a new highway. The bottom layer represents today's members who joined back when the Reverend Ben Harrison was the pastor, the next layer came in during the Reverend Alfred Olson's tenure, the next layer united with this congregation during Dr. Robert Brown's time here, a fourth layer joined more recently during Pastor Carl Javier's service, and the top layer represents those who have come in since the arrival of the present pastor.

While many ministers possess the magnetic personality that immediately wins the loyalty and unreserved support of every one of those layers of members, at least a few do not. The dependable generalization is that the departure of one pastor and the arrival of a successor usually is a disruptive experience. One comparison is with the corporation in which the retiring chief executive officer is succeeded by a younger leader. A better comparison is when the divorced mother of three children, ages eleven to seventeen, brings home a new husband. Occasionally one of those children refuses to give unreserved loyalty, obedience, and affection to the newly arrived stepfather.

Every congregation needs a redundant set of threads of continuity that hold the fellowship together during this transitional period. One thread can be the adult choir. A second thread often is that sacred meeting place. A third may be the hymnal and the familiar liturgy. A fourth usually is that network of loyal volunteer leaders. A fifth may be a powerful denominational identity. In large churches a sixth point of continuity is the paid staff. In small rural churches another may be the cemetery next to the building.

For many congregations, among the most useful components in that redundant network are those lay-led and lay-owned organizations such as the women's organization, the men's fellowship, and the adult Sunday school classes. The Jerusalem Class is one of those threads of continuity in Central Church.

While it is far from the ideal context for learning and retaining content about the Scriptures, the faith, the doctrine, the church, missions, and theology, the Jerusalem Class is a valuable part of the total ministry at Central Church. Its role must be evaluated in terms of relationships, continuity, a responsiveness to human need, and acting out the faith. It should not be evaluated solely in terms of the transmission of doctrinal concepts or an intellectual approach to the Christian faith.

The point of this chapter, however, is not to enter into a divisive discussion on the merits and the limitations of the Jerusalem Class. The point here is to illustrate a second powerful factor when the issue being discussed is expanding the teaching ministry of your church. What are your criteria for evaluation? [2] Without clearly stated criteria that have the consent of a wide slice of the congregation, it will be difficult to agree on which components of the present teaching ministry should be strengthened, which should be enlarged, which should be replaced, which need radical improvement, which need only modest reform, and which need to be supplemented by additional resources.

In other words, what are you trying to do, and what are the criteria you will use in determining how you are doing?

Answering that question requires at least two steps. The first is to agree on goals, on objectives, and on desired future outcomes. The second is to formulate the criteria that will be used to measure progress in meeting those goals. Identifying and agreeing on those criteria for evaluation should rank high on the list of priorities as you seek to expand the teaching ministry of your church. Or, to put it in different words, what are the outcomes you want from your teaching ministry, and how will you measure them?

CHAPTER THREE

A Critical Variable

How important is the role and initiative of the pastor in expanding the teaching ministry of your congregation? A large and growing body of research indicates that the pastor is the number-one variable. This book suggests that the pastor is only one of several influential variables. That may not, however, be a fair statement and does not apply to every Protestant congregation on the North American continent. In the majority of Protestant congregations the skilled, determined, wise, persistent, personable, competent, creative, and persuasive pastor can become the most influential leader in setting priorities, in formulating the desired outcomes of the teaching ministry, in defining the criteria for self-evaluation, and in determining if, where, when, and how the teaching ministry can be expanded.

Rather than debate which is the most influential single variable, it may be more useful to agree that four or five interdependent factors share the top of that list. One is the priority given to the teaching ministry in program planning and in the allocation of scarce resources. A second is the criteria for evaluation. A third is the congregational culture. A fourth is the polity and traditions of that denomination. A fifth is the pastor, but an effective pastor can shape the other four.

The most highly visible example of this principle is the pastor who organizes a new congregation and departs after seventeen years. During those seventeen years this founding pastor exerts tremendous influence in determining the priorities of that congregation, in defining the criteria for self-evaluation, in shaping the culture and traditions of that new mission, and in affirming or rejecting denominational rules and expectations. Once that congregational culture has been formed, it is relatively difficult for the next pastor to change it without the investment of huge quantities of patience, persistence, persuasion, skill, vision, time, and energy, plus the influx of new volunteer leadership.

One example of the power of tradition was described by a seminary professor who spent his formative years in a family who worshiped in a small one-room rural church. There he learned that "Sundayschoolandchurch" was both one word and one experience.[1] The culture of that small congregation taught that a given in life is to participate in both Sunday school and church every Sunday morning. Thus for some readers the beginning point in expanding the teaching ministry of your church may be to examine the congregational culture. Is it supportive of your efforts? Or are the culture and traditions barriers that must be overcome? One example of a congregational culture that is inhospitable to expanding the teaching ministry will be discussed in detail later. This is the schedule that calls for worship and Sunday school to be held concurrently. A second example is the decision of the building committee of 1926 or 1952 or 1978 to construct a meeting place that can accommodate four hundred people in worship and includes only two good classrooms, both for children.

THE INFLUENCE OF SIZE, REGION, AND TURNOVER

Before looking at the pastor's role in the teaching ministry, three cautionary words need to be introduced. Each explains one group of exceptions. The first is that, as a general rule, the larger the size of the congregation, the greater the potential influence of the pastor. In the hundred-year-old congregation that has averaged between thirty and forty at worship for the past six decades, the local traditions, the culture, the schedule, one or two families, the building, and the local theological perspective usually outrank the pastor in formulating policies and priorities. By contrast, in the congregation averaging five hundred or more at worship, the pastor's personality and priorities often top the list of influential factors.

A hundred years ago the Sunday school movement was exceptionally strong in states such as Pennsylvania, Kansas, Iowa, Maryland, North Carolina, Massachusetts, New York, New Jersey, Wisconsin, Indiana, Ohio, and Virginia. Thus it was relatively easy for a Protestant church in the Northeast or Midwest to place a high priority on the Sunday school. The regional context was supportive of that. Today the regional context for expanding the teaching ministry is strongest in the Southeast, Southwest, and West and weakest in the Northeast.

Third, local traditions and the congregational culture tend to be stronger and more resistant to change in those churches with a comparatively low annual turnover in the membership. To be more specific, if the number of confirmed members received each year by adult baptism, confirmation, letter or certificate of transfer, and reaffirmation of faith is less than 5 percent of the total confirmed membership, it is highly likely that culture and tradition will be relatively powerful. If the number of confirmed members received each year by adult baptism, confirmation, letters of transfer, and reaffirmation of faith exceeds 12 percent of the confirmed membership at the beginning of the year, it suggests that (a) this is a numerically growing congregation and (b) tradition and the congregational culture are not powerful barriers to change. The basic generalization is that numerically growing organizations tend to be more receptive to innovation, creativity, new ideas, and change than are numerically shrinking organizations.

CHOICES FOR THE PASTOR

What can a pastor do to expand the teaching ministry of your church?[2] The tremendous differences in gifts, person-alities, tenure, priorities, age, experience, skills, initiative, and productivity among pastors means no one answer fits everyone. The range of possibilities is huge, however, and this can be illustrated by a dozen of the most common examples.

1. The pastor teaches a class in the Sunday school at least forty-five weeks every year plus teaching a weekday or evening class regularly. Modeling is the most powerful pedagogical method, and by teaching, the pastor models the importance of the teaching ministry. Often among the fringe benefits of this are (a) an increase in the supply of volunteer teachers, (b) attractive entry points for future new members, (c) opportunities for meaningful two-way com-munication between parishioner and pastor, (d) increased worship attendance, and (e) the identification of future vol-unteer leaders from among the newer members.

2. The pastor acts as an aggressive advocate for the teaching ministry in preparing the schedule both for Sunday morning and for the entire year.

3. The pastor acts as a strong advocate for the teaching ministry in all stages of policy formulation, in the setting of priorities, and in the allocation of scarce resources (building space, money, time, volunteers, and publicity).

4. The pastor actively staffs the Christian education com-mittee or its equivalent.

5. The pastor accepts an active role in the identification and enlistment of volunteer teachers.

6. The pastor publicizes and promotes attractive continuing education experiences for both volunteer teachers and policy makers in the teaching ministry.

7. If this congregation has a Christian day school or a pre-kindergarten nursery school, the pastor insists that this be conceptualized as one component of the larger teaching ministry of that congregation, not as an isolated and autonomous kingdom or as a community-service program.

8. The pastor urges, and sometimes initiates, the creation of at least one new adult class every year. This is an expression of the old adage, "New groups for new generations."

9. The pastor repeatedly affirms the teaching ministry in general and the volunteer leadership in particular by public prayers, participation in it, pronouncements, celebrations, announcements, and positive comments.

10. The pastor projects high expectations of the teaching ministry. High expectations can be a means of creating the self-fulfilling prophecy. (See chapter 5.)

11. The pastor insists on and assists in a redundant reporting system to the congregation as a whole on the goals, progress, accomplishments, needs, and role of the teaching ministry. Keeping secrets is one of the more effective strategies for undercutting any ministry!

12. Finally, and some will argue this should be at the top of the list of possibilities, the pastor makes the sermon an intentional component of the total teaching ministry. Among the alternatives are (a) expository preaching, (b) scheduling one adult Sunday school class as a "sermon feedback" discussion every week, (c) enlisting a volunteer group of five to seven people to study a specific text for four consecutive Tuesday evenings with the pastor as part of a sermon preparation effort for the sermon to be preached on the second Sunday of the month, with a new group to work on

the text for preparation of the sermon to be preached on the second Sunday of the following month, and so on, (d) a sermon series, (e) preaching from a text that also is the text to be studied by one or more Sunday school classes that Sunday, or (f) mastering and utilizing the skills of "story-telling" as the basic style of preaching.

In scores of congregations that are among the most successful in attracting the generations born after 1955, the sermon is both the centerpiece of the teaching ministry and the number-one reason that these younger adults return Sunday after Sunday for that thirty- to fifty-minute sermon.

The preachers who do this most effectively have mastered the skills of contemporary public discourse, they have recreated the role of the sermon as the number-one channel for transmitting the faith from generation to generation, and they have recaptured the ability of the superb itinerant lecturer or the political figure or the nineteenth century preacher who could capture and hold the attention of a large audience for an hour or two.[3] The number-one enemy of this role of the sermon in the teaching ministry is the person who, after watching a motion picture that grabbed and held the attention of every one of the three hundred people in that theater for ninety minutes, goes over to a coffee shop with friends and announces, "It is ridiculous to expect people to sit comfortably in church for more than an hour, and no preacher can hold people's attention for more than twelve to eighteen minutes."

The rewards for the pastor who accepts this role as a committed leader in the teaching ministry are many. They include the growth in the spiritual maturity of the members, the transformation of the lives of individuals, a broadening of that base of volunteers, a reduction in the normal institutional pressures to place survival goals at the top of the list, an enhancement of loyalty among the members, the creation of attractive and meaningful entry points for newcomers, personal satisfactions, and enrichment of the total life of that nurturing and worshiping community.

For all of that to happen, however, may first require a change in the institutional setting to place ministry, not administration, at the heart of congregational life.

CHAPTER FOUR

What Is the Institutional Context?

Some churches find it easier to expand their teaching ministry than do others. Why? A few of the variables have been discussed earlier. One of the more influential, but more subtle and subjective, is the context or culture. One illustration of this can be found in a recent analysis of "Effective Christian Education" in six large Protestant denominations. The research revealed that by one set of criteria congregations affiliated with the Southern Baptist Convention ranked highest in the integrated faith of the adult members. The parishes affiliated with the Evangelical Lutheran Church in America and the congregations in the United Church of Christ ranked lowest on this scale.[1]

It may not be a coincidence that the Southern Baptist Convention has a long and rich tradition that places a high priority on the teaching ministry of the church in general and on the Sunday school in particular. For many years every congregation affiliated with the Southern Baptist Convention has been asked to submit detailed statistical reports in the uniform letter. Among the many subjects covered in that annual report to Nashville are Sunday school enrollment and average attendance, church training and enrollment, and the enrollment of children and youth in both the women's organization and the men's brotherhood. Until recently, however, that reporting system did not ask for the average attendance at corporate worship. In other words, both the tradition and the polity of the Southern Baptists have reinforced the teaching ministries of congregations. That tradition has made it easy to place a high priority on the teaching ministry in most Southern Baptist churches.

By contrast, in several Lutheran denominations, tradition has placed a high value on education for children and youth, but the teaching ministry with adults has been given a much lower priority. While that tradition has been challenged and changed in hundreds of Lutheran parishes in recent years, the proportion of adults in a structured Bible study group is much lower in an average week in the typical Lutheran parish than it is in the typical Southern Baptist congregation.

For many Lutherans the dominant tradition is still on the centrality of Word and Sacrament, while confirmation often is perceived as graduation from any formal learning program.

Likewise, denominational traditions often place a higher value on the teaching ministry with adults in southern United Methodist and southern Presbyterian congregations than is the pattern in northern churches in those two traditions. In the North, the former Evangelical United Brethren Church placed a higher value on adult Bible study and adult Sunday school classes than was true of former Methodist congregations in the North.

THE LOCAL CONTEXT

In addition to differences in denominational traditions, there are vast differences among congregations. This can be illustrated by two sharply different views of congregational life. In thousands of congregations it appears that the hub of congregational life is the governing board. That is the place where the most influential leaders gather to formulate polity, to determine the priorities in the allocation of scarce resources, and to respond to requests and recommendations from committees.

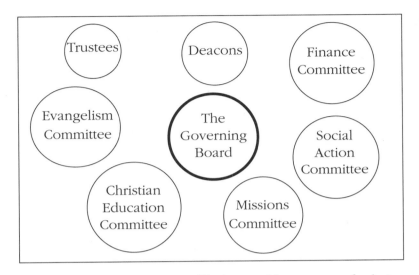

The rest of that picture is filled out with an array of administrative and program committees that are accountable to the governing board. Frequently, the pastor and the church secretary spend considerable time and paper servicing this administrative structure. Some pastors enjoy this more than others do. It is not uncommon for administrative competence to be used as one of the criteria in evaluating the performance of the pastor. Any proposal for expanding the teaching ministry probably will be discussed in terms of the competition for scarce resources, such as the assignment of volunteer workers, money, the pastor's time, building space, schedule, leadership, and creativity. This is a scarcity model of congregational life that often focuses on the competition for the allocation of scarce resources as the central issue in decision-making. This model also encourages frequent references to legalisms, rules, precedents, and tradition. This model also frequently means that the preparation of next year's budget often is an exceptionally influential action.

Only rarely does this model of congregational life offer a

hospitable climate for an expansion of ministry. Thus if the missions committee proposes to raise $15,000 in a special appeal, this may be perceived as a threat to the financial resources available to the trustees or as an intrusion on the authority of the finance committee. This model usually is supportive of the status quo and encourages survival goals to float to the top of the priority list. The administrative committees normally have greater influence than do program committees.

A radically different model of congregational life places the preaching of God's word and the proper administration of the sacraments at the center. In several traditions, prayer, the administration of the Lord's Supper, service, and care of the membership are the top priorities on the time and energy of the lay elders and the deacons. The trustees, the finance committee, and other administrative committees are

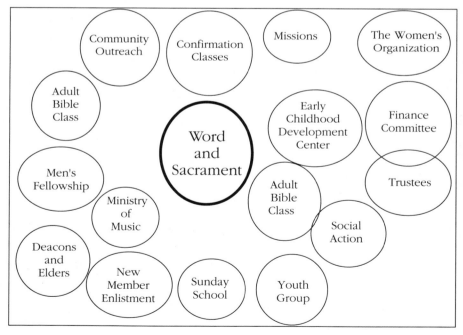

perceived as a means to an end, not as policy making bodies or as central to the life of that congregation.

Surrounding this central focus on word and sacrament are a variety of groups, organizations, classes, ministries, and programs. When someone proposes an expansion of the teaching ministry, the natural response is not competition over scarce resources, but rather which is the logical program group to which this should be assigned for implementation?

Among the most widely used criteria for evaluating the pastor's performance are competence as a preacher, teacher, worship leader, sacramentalist, and initiating leader.

This model usually is receptive to and supportive of goal-oriented approaches to expanding ministry and outreach. Ministry goals, rather than financial limitations, often dominate the decision-making process. This model makes it difficult for institutional survival goals to dominate the goal-setting processes. This is the model of congregational life that normally is most supportive of efforts to expand the teaching ministry.

WHO ARE YOU?

It is true that these two diagrams represent the extreme points on a spectrum reflecting the differences in basic organizing principles for congregational life. Dozens of other models of congregational life can be identified.[2] Most congregations combine elements of three or four or five different models. Another model, for example, finds the life, ministry, priorities, and community image of the congregation to be a reflection of the gifts, skills, experiences, preferences, personality, priorities, productivity, theological position, energy, and worldview of the long-tenured pastor. If that pastor grants a high priority to learning, the teaching ministry is certain to thrive.

A comparison of these two models raises four questions.

1. Which diagram or pattern of congregational life probably will be the most supportive of an expansion of the teaching ministry?

2. Which diagram comes closer to reflecting the dominant pattern or tradition in your congregation?

3. Are you happy with that answer?

4. If not, are you prepared to change it?

If you want to challenge that local tradition, it may be helpful to examine fifteen of the benchmarks that can be found in churches with a positive tradition supporting the teaching ministry.

CHAPTER FIVE

Fifteen Benchmarks

Several years ago the late Virginia Apgar, a well-known physician of her day, developed a simple numerical index to assess the physical condition of a newborn baby. The Apgar score is a summary of (1) heart rate, (2) respiratory effort, (3) muscle tone, (4) reflex irritability, and (5) the color of the newborn. The five-minute score is considered by physicians to be a good predictor of an infant's chances for survival and long-term health status. Since 1983 the Apgar scores at one and five minutes after birth have been reported by forty-six states and the District of Columbia. In 1988 42.1 percent of all children scored high (9 or 10) on the Apgar scale one minute after birth, down from 49 percent ten years earlier. Newborns of mothers age 25-34 years are most likely to have high Apgar scores.

In a similar manner it is possible to identify a variety of factors that are found in most churches with an effective teaching ministry. The first, of course, is that the leaders place a high priority on the teaching ministry. A second, which was discussed in chapter 2, is that the leaders also have agreed on a set of outcomes and know how to evaluate what is happening. A third, which many insist is the most influential single variable, is that the pastor is an active advocate of and deeply involved in the teaching ministry. A fourth is that the institutional context is oriented toward ministry rather than toward institutional survival goals. Several other variables are discussed in subsequent chapters.

The purpose of this chapter is to identify fifteen other benchmarks or factors that can be used as you evaluate and seek to expand the teaching ministry of your congregation.

The first three are the most subjective, the most controversial, and the most difficult to measure.

THE NUMBER-ONE QUESTION

A three-and-one-half year study of Christian education in six denominations concluded that "The primary aim of congregational life is to nurture . . . a vibrant, life-changing faith, the kind of faith that shapes one's way of being, thinking and acting."[1] This became the benchmark for evaluating the effectiveness of formal Christian education ministries. These researchers also concluded that the teaching ministry possesses great potential for renewing congregational life and for reversing the numerical decline of the congregation.

Out of this study comes the first benchmark of an excellent teaching ministry. The quality of the teaching ministry can be measured by a two-part question. Does the teaching ministry of your congregation result in the transformation of the lives of the participants and in helping people grow in the faith? Is that the number-one outcome you seek? Is the teaching ministry designed to help make that happen?

MUTUAL REINFORCEMENT

A second benchmark of an excellent teaching ministry is that it is consistent with and reinforces the doctrinal position, the theological stance, the values, and the priorities in life that are advocated by that congregation.

To state it in simple terms, the same doctrinal stance, the same approach to the Holy Scriptures, and the same definition of the role of the worshiping community will be taught in every classroom as is taught from the pulpit or is expressed by actions of the governing board. This does not mean a lock step approach to every facet of the faith, but it does mean the teachers, the governing board, the program committees, and the minister share a common understanding of the Christian faith.

A simple way to describe it is to divide the theological spectrum into five segments with one segment representing the broad middle, two on the conservative side of the middle, and two on the liberal side. Ideally the policymakers, the teachers, and the minister share space in the same segment, although some may be at one end of that segment while a few may have one foot in an adjacent segment in the other direction. It is difficult to believe that it will not be disruptive if the minister and three or four teachers place themselves in the segment at one extreme end of that spectrum while several policymakers and three or four teachers identify themselves with the segment at the opposite end of that spectrum. The teaching ministry of one congregation may be able to cover 30 to 40 percent of that spectrum, but not the entire spectrum.

In other words, internal consistency and coherence is another important benchmark of an excellent teaching ministry.

WHAT DO WE TALK ABOUT?

Some will argue that the third of these first three benchmarks should be at the top of the list. An excellent teaching ministry enables and encourages people to talk with one another about their faith questions. This includes lively discussions about the faith and how one lives out the faith at meetings of the governing board and in committee meetings as well as in the classroom, in the home, at social gatherings, at work, while on vacation, and in the kitchen.

A strong argument can be made that the most important

benchmark of an excellent teaching ministry is that it enables people to articulate their faith more clearly. The better people are able to articulate what they believe, the easier it is to move ahead on that faith journey, to share that faith with others, to respond to the questions of inquirers (including children), and to grow in the faith. Obviously that process is facilitated if the minister, the teachers, and all policymakers are both skilled and comfortable when talking about what they believe as Christians.

SELF-FULFILLING EXPECTATIONS

One of the four or five most influential benchmarks to be discussed in this chapter is also one of the most subtle and subjective. What are your expectations? To a substantial degree expectations tend to be self-fulfilling. For example, the congregation that offers Sunday school at the same hour as worship attracts a lot of families seeking that one-hour convenience package. Another example is the church that has a strong adult division in the Sunday school, which usually attracts a larger number of children than the congregation that offers no adult classes. (See chapter 10.)

The expectation to be discussed here has many facets, four of which illustrate the central point.

In a growing number of congregations the Sunday morning schedule has been designed to encourage people to come for three or four periods. One example enables adults to come for breakfast, participate in an adult class, teach in the children's division during the Sunday school hour, and share in corporate worship in the fourth period. Another example is the schedule that encourages teachers to be in an adult class at either the first or third hour, participate in worship at either the first or third hour, and teach during the middle hour. For most people, however, the expectation is that they will be in both worship and Sunday school. The choice is between worship followed by Sunday school or Sunday school followed by worship.

A second facet is the adult new-member class. A few churches still receive adults without asking them to participate in any preparatory class. Many more, however, offer a one-hour to six-session new member class. A growing number of churches combine five goals. The first is to offer a more thorough grounding in the faith to prospective new members. A second is to facilitate the assimilation of new members and reduce the number of new members who disappear soon after joining. A third goal is to help prospective new members fully understand both what this congregation offers to people and what is expected of the members. The fourth goal is to help the veteran leaders become better acquainted with the new members and vice versa. A fifth goal is to help new members meet and make new friends in that fellowship.

The facet of the teaching ministry designed to achieve these goals is the thirty-six- or forty-two- or forty-five-week new-member class. This weekly class is led for the entire period by a team of three volunteer leaders, one or two of whom are officers in that congregation. The classes are taught by volunteer specialists. One specialist may teach a four-week introduction to the Christian faith. Another may teach a six-week introduction to the Bible. A third may teach a four-week introduction to that denomination. A fourth may teach a five-week course on doctrine. A fifth may take five sessions of the class to go over the history, role, and priorities of this congregation. Someone else spends three weeks on Christian stewardship. Another teacher may take three to seven weeks to explain the various ministries of this church and to discuss the opportunities for volunteer involvement in ministry. Another teacher may devote two or three weeks to polity and governance. The subject matter varies from church to church as does the length of each unit. This use of volunteer specialists for the teaching ministry enables each one to master a single subject, provides the members of the class with a change of pace, gives several teachers an opportunity to meet these newcomers, and does not overload any one teacher.

Usually the pastor spends three or four sessions with each class. One class may meet on Saturday mornings, the next one begins two months later and meets on Tuesday evenings, and a third begins six weeks later and meets during the Sunday school hour.

Occasionally one of these classes refuses to end when the members unite with that church and continues for years as an adult Sunday school class with a passing parade of members.

A third facet of the self-fulfilling expectation has become increasingly common since 1960. This is the intensive, systematic, comprehensive, and demanding adult Bible study program. Most of these meet for two to three hours once a week for thirty-six to forty-eight weeks a year and run for two to four years. Bethel, Kerygma, Trinity, Bible Study Fellowship, Crossways, SEARCH, and Disciple are among the more widely used programs.

When first proposed, a typical response conveys this discouraging message: "That might work in some churches, but it wouldn't work here! Our people are too busy, some of them travel for a living, we have a lot of older people who are here only part of the year, most of the women are employed outside the home, our older members won't come out after dark, so many of our parents have to take their kids to soccer games and other activities, we now have a growing number of members who hold two or three jobs, and, of course, the single parent could never make it."

When those discouraging words are taken seriously, the proposal usually is dropped and forgotten. When high expectations are projected, the common result is a surprisingly large enrollment with relatively few dropping out before the end of that long journey.

A fourth facet of self-fulfilling expectations is found in the debate over the summer slump. One side of this debate is represented by those who argue, "You can't expect the teachers to teach fifty-two Sundays a year! They need a vacation. Likewise a lot of our families will be on vacation during the summer and won't be around. Let's cut back to one adult class and one class for children for the summer. We'll be lucky if we get a total of thirty-five people for the two combined." That point of view prevails, and Sunday school attendance drops from an average of over three hundred in April to thirty in August. The prophecy is fulfilled.

The other side of this story is represented by the churches that depend on teams of three to five teachers for each class and maintain the same Sunday morning schedule for fifty-two weeks a year. The only significant changes they make are: (1) each Sunday during the summer is designed as a separate free-standing "lesson" rather than as one session in a six- or thirteen-week sequence so people who missed the previous Sunday will not feel "left out in the dark" and first-time visitors will not have to play "catchup"; (2) an aggressive direct-mail campaign is run all summer, directed at new residents to the community and to people who do not go to church anywhere to come and find a church home here; and (3) every special Sunday has a special theme for the worship service, designed to attract first-time visitors.[2] The typical result is that Sunday school attendance in August is up slightly over the April average. The expectation is fulfilled.

The expectations your leaders project will be one of the most influential factors as you seek to expand the teaching ministry of your church.

WHAT DOES THE SCHEDULE SAY?

Overlapping self-fulfilling expectations is a subject that deserves special attention. This is the schedule. What does the schedule say about the importance of the teaching ministry? Does the schedule, perhaps subtly but consistently, undercut the teaching ministry? Three examples will illustrate one such pattern.

"I hope you won't be offended when some of us get up and walk out while you're talking," apologizes a member of an adult class to the visiting teacher that Sunday morning, "but we have to go and robe and warm up with the choir."

"We never have Sunday school on Easter," explained a veteran leader to the newly arrived pastor. "We have such big crowds on Easter that we have to hold two services, so we just cut out Sunday school."

"On the third Sunday of every month we ask the Cherub Choir to sing in the worship service," explained the superintendent to a new teacher, "so about half of your class will be late arriving on those Sundays. They leave the service during the hymn before the sermon and go to their class."

The clear message in all three of these comments is (a) Sunday school has a secondary role in relationship to worship and (b) the schedule has been designed to make sure everyone knows and repeatedly is reminded of what comes first and what is of secondary importance.

If the goal is to expand the teaching ministry, and if one part of the strategy to attain that goal is to strengthen the Sunday school, a useful beginning point is the schedule.

Ideally a ninety-minute period of time will be reserved for the Sunday school with zero competition during the sixty minutes in the middle of that block of time.

A widely used schedule illustrates this.

8:30 A.M. Worship
9:45 A.M. Sunday school
11:00 A.M. Worship

The combination of fellowship and providing people time to move from one place to another is allotted fifteen minutes. Sunday school classes have a full sixty minutes before anyone has to leave a class for another responsibility. This is critically important for the individual who is the sole teacher of a Sunday school class for children and also sings in the chancel choir at the second service.

In several larger congregations where parking congestion adds to the problem, the schedule allows thirty minutes between Sunday school and the second worship service.

   8:15 A.M. Worship
   9:30 A.M. Sunday school
 11:00 A.M. Worship

In the West and Southwest everything on this schedule may be moved up fifteen to thirty minutes.

   7:00 A.M. Breakfast
   7:15 A.M. One adult class meets until 9:00 A.M.
   8:00 A.M. Worship plus rehearsal of the choir that sings at the second service
   9:15 A.M. Sunday school
 10:45 A.M. Worship

One of the more effective ways of undercutting the Sunday school is to offer Sunday school and worship at the same hour so each is in direct competition with the other for people's time. Another is this schedule.

   9:00 A.M. Worship
 10:00 A.M. Sunday school
 11:00 A.M. Worship

This may appear to be a highly efficient schedule, but it tends to reduce the opportunities for fellowship and to undermine the Sunday school. It also makes it nearly impossible for the pastor to teach in the Sunday school.

Who speaks for the Sunday school when you design your Sunday morning schedule?

A second way to use the schedule to undermine the teaching ministry is to place the top priority on board and committee meetings when making out the schedule for next year. The trustees may meet on the third Monday of every month, the governing board meets on the second Tuesday, the officers of the women's organization meet on the first Wednesday evening, and every Thursday evening calls for the meeting of at least one program committee. A couple of ad hoc committees pick a Monday or Tuesday evening, and the finance committee always meets on the Tuesday evening before the monthly meeting of the board. The result is that no one evening is attractive to everyone for that new weekly evening Bible study class. This also inhibits the role of the pastor as a teacher.

The obvious solution is to reserve Tuesday and Wednesday evenings of every week for the teaching ministry and let the administrative and program committees choose among the remaining evenings.

Another way to use the schedule to undercut the teaching ministry can be seen when a new design for Sunday morning is prepared for the summer. This often calls for either cutting back on the time available for the teaching ministry by squeezing Sunday school and worship into a shorter block of time or running a reduced Sunday school or "learning center" concurrently with worship.

While this may not sound believable to some readers, in hundreds of communities several churches will cut back on Sunday school during the summer. They do this despite the data that reveal two-thirds of the families moving into that community do so between mid-May and mid-September. That means the peak of the church shopping season often falls in August, just before the public schools open, and coincides with the period of least activity in those churches where the leaders wonder, "I don't see why our church doesn't grow. There are so many more people living here now, why can't our church reach some of them?"

THE ROLE OF MUSIC

One of the benchmarks of a good teaching ministry is to go beyond the written and spoken word to communicate the gospel. Among the most effective tools for doing this is music. Perhaps the most widespread use of music in communicating the good news is that simple hymn "Jesus Loves Me." Close behind is the popularity of "Amazing Grace."

Strengthen the ingredient of your teaching ministry called music. Sing a hymn near the beginning and/or close of that Tuesday evening Bible class. Encourage each adult Sunday school class to compose their own special hymn that will be sung when the class meets. Enlist someone with a guitar or keyboard or accordian who will visit every class in the children's division of the Sunday school every week and teach the children new hymns. Organize a Sunday school band or orchestra that plays on thirty occasions every year. Use music to help children memorize the books of the Bible and meaningful verses.

In many larger congregations this is facilitated by assigning the two portfolios of the teaching ministry and music to the same staff member.

WHAT IS SPECIAL ABOUT TODAY?

Most Christian congregations experience their peak worship attendance of the year on Easter Sunday. For others the peak is Christmas Eve. For a few it is the last Sunday for the retiring pastor or the first Sunday for the new minister. For some it is Rally Day in the fall. Occasionally it may be Palm Sunday because Easter coincides with the vacation schedule of the local public schools. For a handful every year the biggest crowd of the year occurs when the summer homecoming weekend coincides with the celebration of the one hundredth anniversary of the founding of that parish. In an even smaller number the peak crowd of that year may come when their long-tenured pastor who was just elected to the episcopacy is installed as a bishop.

The point of these illustrations is that special occasions draw big crowds. This one component of a larger strategy to expand the teaching ministry could be to conceptualize every class, event, experience, group, and program as special. One example of this is to invite the former pastor who returned to this community to retire to teach a new Thursday evening Bible study group. A second is the special six-week study program offered every year during Lent. A third, and one of the most common, is that special class taught by the pastor every Sunday morning. Even more common is Rally Day as the special day that marks the beginning of a new Sunday school year. One of the more traditional practices, now widely abandoned, is the opening exercise that includes the celebration of birthdays that fall in this week. For most of us, "my birthday" is a special day. Other examples include the six-week Tuesday evening class to coincide with the birthday of the founder of that denomination, the Friday evening crowd that turns out to celebrate the end of Vacation Bible School, the carefully designed three-Sunday focus on the churches' response to world hunger that is the theme of every Sunday school class for those three weeks, the special four-week class held annually for training new teachers, and the new adult class launched every July for newlyweds.

The central dynamic occurs when the individual is invited, and the immediate response is, "Hey, that sounds just like it was designed for me!"

OUR NEED OR YOURS?

"We need at least five more members if we are going to make this new class a success. Please, won't you join us?" That widely heard plea is one route to follow in expanding the teaching ministry. A fair number of people do feel a need to be needed. Sometimes this plea does produce additional recruits, but too often they depart after a month or two.

A better approach is to begin with the needs of the people you are seeking to reach and serve. (CAUTION: Some readers may express strong disagreement with this approach and may want to skip this section! Their perspective declares that everyone needs to hear the good news and to accept Jesus Christ as Lord and Savior. Any deviation from that as the top priority or the suggestion of a different beginning point is perceived as a concession to the culture or yielding to a consumer orientation or, more precisely, as heresy. One response to that criticism is that Jesus repeatedly asked people where they hurt and began the conversation with the hurt of that individual who was meeting Jesus for the first time. By contrast, Jesus often used a different beginning point when speaking to crowds.)

Those churches able and willing to explore this alternative can reach large numbers of people who today are not actively involved in the life of any worshiping community.

One variation on this approach is to create mutual support or self-help groups. Typically the "curriculum" combines the message of the gospel with what has been learned by leaders in the helping professions. This often means the evangelical churches are more likely to organize these mutual support groups than are the more liberal congregations that choose to build new groups around a cause rather than in response to the needs of the individual.

Among the more rapidly growing examples of this

expression of the teaching ministry are mutual support groups designed for (1) the adult children of an alcoholic parent, (2) parents of gays and lesbians, (3) adults who as teenagers experienced the loss created by the divorce of their parents, (4) recently widowed mature adults, (5) parents who have experienced the death of a child within the past year or so (Compassionate Friends is a secular version of this), (6) new mothers who, after a decade or more in the labor force, no longer are employed outside the home and now are full-time homemakers, (7) people going through a traumatic divorce experience, (8) young widows, (9) newlyweds who are both embarking on their second or subsequent marriage, (10) new empty-nest couples, (11) parents of developmentally disabled children, and (12) newlyweds in an interfaith marriage.[3]

The crucial factor in making these mutual support groups successful experiences for the participants is highly competent leadership! This requirement may be one reason why the vast majority of congregations have ignored this demand and secular groups have come in to fill the vacuum.

Several surveys suggest that if a congregation seeks to be responsive to the needs of members (which is a different focus than attempting to attract those not actively involved in the life of any congregation), the top five priorities in the teaching ministry with adults should be (1) helping people in their desire to know more about what the Bible says, (2) enabling people to deepen their personal relationship with Jesus, (3) assisting adults in applying their faith to everyday life, (4) responding to members' desire to learn how to better express their love and concern for others, and (5) providing guidance in making better decisions on moral questions.

In some parishes the response is to offer short-term classes that focus on one of these five concerns for three to six months. In other churches these and similar questions become the central theme for three to six months in one or more continuing classes. In others these five concerns are part of the agenda of every mutual support group.

STRENGTHEN INTERGENERATIONAL RELATIONSHIPS

"We expect the kids to work and earn the money to pay for the tickets," explained the pastor of a California church. "We do not allow the parents to pay for their own tickets! That is one of the critical dynamics that makes this work."

This pastor was explaining the annual Parent Appreciation Banquet sponsored by the high school youth group. All parents of youth in that program are invited to a catered seven-course dinner. The meal is served by the youth. The program for the evening follows the meal. One-by-one these young people come out, stand before the group, and express in varying degrees of detail their appreciation for what their parents have done for them. Some of the youth do this with a memorized speech. Others do it extemporaneously. A few simply write a letter of thanks to their parent or parents and hand it to the parent, but usually a couple of these, with the strength gained from peer support, are able to call on a previously unknown reservoir of courage and read it.

In today's world at least a few teenagers have had zero practice in articulating their gratitude to their parents. This highly structured event provides that practice. Like most of us, these youth subsequently are more comfortable doing what they have had practice in doing.

Other examples of strengthening intergenerational relationships through the teaching ministry include: (1) asking a high school class to design, write, and teach a course on what the Bible says to today's Christians for an adult class in the Sunday school; (2) organizing a Surrogate Grandfathers' Club, which is the number-one support system, lobby, and aide to the weekday Early Childhood Development

Center; (3) creating a combination Bible study-quilting group for mature women who enjoy quilting and younger women who want to learn to quilt while an expert teacher leads the discussion that can be carried on while quilting; (4) organizing a Sunday school orchestra or band that plays at all special events (this was very common in the first quarter of this century); and (5) creating a special fifteen-week intergenerational adult class that worships with a church from a different tradition on one Sabbath out of three. The following Sunday is spent discussing the previous week's experience. The next Sunday is preparation for the next visit. This often is an attractive learning experience for teenagers and adults of all ages. In today's world it is not uncommon for one or two of the adults to have grown up in the religious tradition being visited on a particular Sabbath. The central dynamic is that shared experiences constitute one of the most effective means of building friendships.

REPLACEMENTS OR PIONEERS?

"I understand we will be receiving nine adults as new members of this church later this morning," commented the teacher of an adult class to the pastor a few minutes before the beginning of the Sunday school hour. "I hope you can persuade at least three or four of them to join our class. When I began teaching this class nine years ago, our attendance ran between twenty-five and thirty. This past year it was down to an average of eleven. If we don't get some new members pretty soon, our class will simply disappear."

These comments raise three questions. The first, which will not be discussed here, is perhaps that the time has come to find a new teacher for that class.

A second, which is discussed in chapter 10, is over who should recruit new members for long-established classes.

The third concerns expectations projected on new members. Should they be expected to provide the needed replacements to extend the life expectancy of existing classes? Or is it wiser and more effective to ask these new members to help pioneer new classes?

The second best answer is to encourage or require new members to join existing classes. This often is seen as part of a larger strategy for socializing and assimilating the newcomers into the life, culture, and friendship circles of that congregation. The second best response is to encourage new members to help pioneer new classes, groups, choirs, events, cells, circles, and ad hoc task forces. This is consistent with the injunction, "New groups for new people."

The best answer is to offer at least two or three choices. Adult new members are invited to (1) help pioneer a new class and/or (2) join a teaching team that needs a new member and/or (3) enroll in a teacher-training program and/or (4) serve on an administrative or program standing committee of the teaching ministry and/or (5) serve on a special task force that is being established to expand the teaching ministry and/or (6) serve as one of two or three volunteer leaders who will create a new class and/or (7) join an existing class.

Do not offer the either-or choice of "Please join the group to which we assign you, or do not participate in our teaching ministry."

VISUAL OR VERBAL?

"What did you do in Sunday school this morning?" asked the mother of her eight-year-old son as they drove home after their first Sunday at Trinity Church.

"We sat in a circle, and the teacher read stories to us," came the reply.

"Did you enjoy it?" inquired the mother.

"It was boring," replied the son mournfully as he used one of his favorite words.

———————

"Hey, Mom!" exclaimed the eight-year-old boy as he raced over to his mother after Sunday school on their first day at Salem Church. "Do you know what we're doing in Sunday school? We're making a movie! Today I was a Roman soldier, and next week I'm going to get to operate the camcorder! I can't wait till next Sunday. I wish we had a camcorder. We are coming back here next Sunday, aren't we? I promised the teachers I would be back. This is the church we're going to join, isn't it?"

Which of these two eight-year-old boys will be back for a second Sunday in that class next week?

In another congregation the second grade Sunday school class has five electronic sketchpads and one television receiver. After listening to a teacher read a Bible story, each one of the five second graders in that corner for that twenty-minute period creates a picture on an electronic sketchpad to illustrate what he or she perceived to be the central message of the story. With the help of the teacher, these images are transmitted one-by-one and are shown to the entire group on the screen of the television set in full color. At the end of this twenty-minute period, these five join another teacher in another corner of the room for a different experience and five other second graders come over to listen to a story and to interpret it visually. The teacher can record all these images on a videotape and use that tape the following week as a combination refresher-reinforcement experience. Modern technology also makes it possible for one of those teachers to take the videotape to the room where the parents of those children are meeting and show it while explaining to the parents what the children have been learning.

Electronic teaching aids already are widely used in public school classrooms, and the research suggests children find them easier to master than books. Today's children and youth have grown up in a television era filled with color. Whether we approve of it or not, television probably will be with us for several more years.

As you seek to expand the teaching ministry of your congregation, will you rely largely on the printed and spoken word, or will you place a greater emphasis on the visual communication of the gospel?

OBLIGATION OR ENJOYABLE EXPERIENCE?

Overlapping that is a related question. Do participants in the teaching ministry of your church regard this as an obligation they owe God? Or do they look forward to their continued involvement?

The Jerusalem Class for adults, described in the opening pages of the second chapter, attracts people because they want to be there. Friendship ties, caring, mutual support, love, and the opportunity to be with people who display a deep affection for one another are at least as powerful as the content to be studied in bringing these adults together every Sunday morning.

The mutual support groups identified in a previous section of this chapter draw participants because that group provides a response to a need that has long been neglected.

The combination of a chance to express their creativity and to learn in a highly visual approach to education draws the children in the two Sunday school classes described in the previous page.

As you seek to expand your teaching ministry, do not concentrate exclusively on the content to be transmitted. Build in the factors that make people want to return to the next meeting of this group. Learning can be fun! The context for learning can be one that attracts people or it can be one that repels folks. Try to build in a redundant set of factors that will motivate people to return next week. Don't put all of your eggs in that basket labeled "obligation."

WORKING WITH OR AGAINST THE REAL ESTATE?

"How can anyone expect us to offer a closely graded Sunday school for children and to provide lots of choices for adults when all we have are two rooms? One is the upstairs sanctuary, and one is the basement," laments the Sunday school superintendent in the eighty-member congregation that has been meeting in a small white frame building next to the cemetery since 1893.

The answer, of course, is that is not a reasonable expectation. A common response is to use curtains to divide the basement into six rooms and place a teacher with two or three children in each room. The curtains may be effective visual barriers, but the sound comes through and is a disruptive part of the learning environment. The youth meet in the chancel, with the adult class meeting in the rear pews, and they distract each other visually as well as by sounds.

Working against the design of the meeting place makes it difficult to carry on an effective teaching ministry. One alternative could be to install a movable sound barrier wall that would divide either the upstairs or the downstairs room and organize the Sunday school around three intergenerational classes. A second would be to schedule the classes for adults at another time. A third would be to merge with two other small congregations and construct a new meeting place at a new site under a new name with new leadership as part of a larger strategy for a fresh start for the next century of ministry. A fourth would be to schedule the children's Sunday school for Saturday mornings and design two or three classes for youth and adults for Sunday morning. A fifth would be to remodel the building. A sixth could be to add a home-study component to the teaching ministry for both children and adults rather than to attempt to do it all on Sunday morning. A seventh would be to schedule part of the teaching ministry for Wednesday evening and part for Sunday morning. An eighth alternative could be to design a three-hour schedule for Sunday morning with worship in the middle. Sunday school for families with children would be scheduled at the first hour. Youth and adults would meet for study during the third hour.

These alternatives are not offered as "solutions," but rather to illustrate the basic point. Do you work with the building or against it? Is the building an enemy, or can it be made into an ally?

In one larger congregation the building was designed to house Sunday school departments. Each department included one large room in the middle with three tiny rooms on each side. Fifty years after the building was completed, a team of four creative teachers made this into a perfect facility for team teaching a class of nearly thirty fifth and sixth graders. The room, which had been designed to house six small classes for grades one through six with opening and closing exercises in that big middle room, was ideal for an interest group approach to team teaching one large class.

As you seek to expand the teaching ministry of your church, can the real estate be made into an ally? Or is it an implacable foe? If it is the enemy, who will win the war?

CONTEMPORARY STANDARDS OF QUALITY

"I remember when I was a teenager Mr. Swanson taught the high school class in the coal room," recalled Ben Roberts, a seventy-seven-year-old lifetime member of the Hillside Church. "It was dirty, we burned coal in those days, but we got by. And let me tell you, it was hot in there in the summertime! Mr. Swanson was an excellent teacher, a great disciplinarian, and the perfect model of a committed Christian. I don't see why we have to spend a half-million dollars on a new children's wing. The kids of today are spoiled! Why spend all that money for rooms that will be used only a few hours a week?"

Is that a necessary expenditure? Maybe yes, maybe no. If all the teenagers in your congregation were born back in 1915 or 1916, it probably is unnecessary to provide new high quality space for them. If, however, you are seeking to reach and serve children born during the past fifteen years, you may want to use a different set of criteria. Instead of using the reminiscences of the older pillars of the church as the standard for evaluating the physical facilities, it might be wiser to visit the public schools, shopping malls, and other gathering places inhabited by today's children and youth. Many of these have indoor plumbing, electrical lighting, and air that is heated or cooled to produce a comfortable temperature.

If your goal is to expand the teaching ministry by reaching and serving people born after 1960, it may be necessary to have better quality physical facilities than if your number-one target is to serve people born before 1960. Sometimes new facilities will be an influential factor in determining who comes back next week.

MONEY DOESN'T BUY HAPPINESS, BUT . . .

As mentioned earlier, the expectations of the leaders, the support of the pastor, and local traditions are crucial variables. They do not cost money. If, however, you are serious about expanding the teaching ministry, you probably will have to increase the level of expenditures. In many churches that will be chiefly for capital improvements. In a few, the increased expenditures may be largely for staff. For most churches, expansion means more money for materials, equipment, in-service training of teachers, publicity as you invite nonmembers to come and share in your feast, expanded custodial services, furniture, and higher utility costs.

To be more precise, if you plan to double the number of participants in your teaching ministry, you should expect to enhance the quality of the total program, and that may mean quadrupling expenditures. Happiness can come cheap, but education costs money!

While this is far from an exhaustive listing of all the benchmarks of an excellent teaching ministry, these do offer a beginning point for self-evaluation and for developing a strategy to make the institutional context a more hospitable environment for learning. A crucial component of that strategy is agreeing on a definition of the client for your teaching ministry.

CHAPTER SIX

Who Is the Client?

High on that list of issues to be considered when planning to expand the teaching ministry of your church is a fundamental question. Who is the number-one client?

Back when the sermon was the heart of the teaching ministry, the identification of the number-one client was a choice among three alternatives. Is the number-one client for that sermon today's members? Or is the number-one client the unsaved and the unchurched? Or should the number-one client be the children who will be the carriers of the faith in the next generation?

In recent years the answer to this question has been more difficult to define. If one looks at the programs offered by denominational agencies and by theological seminaries, one would see that it would be easy to persuade a visitor from another planet that the number-one client is the parish pastor who presumably has graduated from seminary.

If one retraces the history of the scores of parachurch organizations that were created between 1940 and 1990, one finds that most of them emerged to service individuals, especially high school aged youth, college and university students, and women. Their number-one client was the individual. The immense numbers who responded suggest these clients were not being serviced adequately by congregations. The parachurch organizations emerged to fill a vacuum. Most came into existence with teaching as their central reason for being. Some, such as the Bethel Bible study program, were designed to reinforce the teaching ministry of parishes and to supplement what was being done by denominational agencies. Others, such as Bible Study Fellowship, built their own following, even at the risk of being seen as competitors of pastors and congregations.

If one reviews the early history of the Sunday school movement, one finds that the earliest clients were drawn largely from the children of parents who were not church members. The number-one client was the child who worked and/or was on the streets for six days a week. The First Day Society in Philadelphia in 1791 made it clear that the number-one client was "the offspring of indigent parents . . . previously to their being apprenticed to trades."[1]

If one looks at the churches that placed a high priority on confirmation classes as a central component of the teaching ministry of the parish, it is clear that the primary clients were children of members, not urchins off the street.

If one visits those churches that include a Christian day school running through at least grade six, it may appear the number-one client consists of the children of members. This often is reflected in a comparatively low tuition charge for children from member families and a much higher tuition for children from non-member households. In other parishes, however, it quickly becomes apparent that the number-one client is the entire family with children of elementary school age, not solely the children. That Christian day school may be the most visible and the most costly of these programs, but it is only one of a constellation of ministries, programs, classes, events, experiences, choirs, groups, circles, and parties designed for the family. The entire package may include two dozen or more components such as parenting classes, father-daughter roller skating parties, a circle in the women's organization for mothers of children in that school, two or three children's choirs, athletic teams, one or two adult Sunday school classes for parents of elementary school aged children, divorce recovery workshops, a circle in the women's organization for single-parent mothers of elementary school aged children, a family camping weekend once or twice a year, a pre-kindergarten nursery school, an intergenerational orchestra, and a surrogate grandfathers' club as part of the school's support system.

"We have such a hard time recruiting teachers for the Sunday school, we give them a lot of freedom in what they teach and how they teach," explained the superintendent of the Sunday school in a congregation averaging 110 at worship and 60 in the Sunday school. "My primary responsibility is to make sure there is an adult in every classroom every week at least a couple of minutes before the beginning of the Sunday school hour. It is hard enough getting people to teach today that I don't try to interfere in what they do or how they do it."

Is the number-one client in this Sunday school the superintendent or the teachers?

In one large church reporting over a thousand members, the number of cribs in the nursery was reduced from five to two, despite the fact that four of the most active volunteers in the congregation were pregnant and one was carrying twins. The explanation was that the nursery looked neater, cleaner, less cluttered, and more attractive with fewer cribs. The rule of thumb in determining how many cribs will be needed in the nursery is one crib for each one hundred members. That number may be adjusted upward or downward depending on the age of the members, the age and marital status of the people that congregation is seeking to attract, the Sunday morning schedule, the nature of the weekday program, and the value system of the leaders.

In this example it appears the number-one client for the nursery consists of people who will look in at it rather than the mothers who will use it.

In a couple of dozen very large congregations this question of the number-one client was settled soon after the arrival of the new senior minister. It quickly became apparent to anyone who studied the situation that the number-one client of the teaching ministry is composed of the church shoppers, seekers, searchers, sojourners, and pilgrims who meet in the largest available meeting room in an adult class taught by the new senior minister in the period between the close of the first worship service and the beginning of the second service. This class receives the greatest quantity of publicity in the weekly advertisement in the local newspaper, it is the only Sunday school class identified in the Yellow Pages of the telephone directory, and it receives more space than any other aspect of the teaching ministry in the monthly mailing to new residents. Clearly prospective future new members constitute the number-one client in the teaching ministry of these churches!

In scores of larger churches an influential client of the teaching ministry is the highly competent, learned, enthusiastic, articulate, gifted, and aggressive associate minister who is scheduled to preach on only three or four Sundays a year. The teaching ministry gives this minister a chance to utilize gifts and skills that only rarely are permitted to be displayed from the pulpit.

In many of the churches that are attracting large numbers of adults from the generations born after World War II, the teaching ministry has been designed to make them the number-one client. The typical program in these congregations includes a strong adult division with excellent teachers in the Sunday school, plus adult classes offered on a regular basis three or four days or evenings through the week.

In a small but growing number of larger congregations the obvious number-one client of the teaching ministry consists of the adults who sign up to be in a new member orientation class. The typical class runs from 36 to 45 weeks, and a new one is organized every month or two. One meets on Tuesday evenings, another on Saturday mornings, a third during the Sunday school hour, and a fourth may meet on Sunday evening or Wednesday evening. These classes often meet in the most attractive available room, they are led by several of the most competent and committed volunteer leaders in the congregations, the pastor or senior minister spends more time with these classes than with any other facet of the teaching ministry, and they receive more publicity than any other aspect of the total teaching ministry.

Back in the 1970s and 1980s a common practice was to identify as the number-one client the parents of young children who wanted the "one-hour package" that enabled the parents to be in worship while their children attended Sunday school. This schedule had far greater appeal to the parents born in 1944 or 1949 or 1953 than it has to the parents born after 1955. Most of the church-going parents from this post-1955 generation prefer a schedule that includes attractive and meaningful learning experiences for adults as well as for children.

In at least a few churches this debate evokes two responses. The pastor declares the number-one client for the Sunday school should be the volunteers who supervise, staff, design, and worry about the Sunday school. "If they feel they own it and run it, they'll do a good job," asserts this minister. "Therefore I stay away and don't interfere."

These lay volunteers contend that the number-one client is this minister who wants to be left alone and not be bothered with the Sunday school.

In several traditions the number-one client for the teaching ministry always has been children and youth. Typically, the Sunday school and the confirmation classes are the two highly visible expressions of this priority.

In countless churches the rhetoric proclaims the number-one priority is children and youth. "They represent the future of the church!" A visit to the Sunday school, however,

77

reveals that the two best meeting rooms are used by adult classes, and the least attractive room houses the junior high class and the next worst is the nursery. In identifying that number-one client, do you listen to the rhetoric or examine the practices?

WHAT IS THE ISSUE?

This broad range of examples is offered to illustrate one relatively simple but exceedingly crucial point: You cannot get there from here unless you know where you are going. The translation of that ancient bit of wisdom is equally simple. It is difficult to prepare and implement a plan to expand the teaching ministry of your church unless you are able to agree on the principal clients. After that agreement has been achieved, it is relatively easy to make decisions on the allocation of space, on the schedule, on the priorities in the allocation of the time and energy of volunteers, on curriculum, on staffing, on the allocation of financial resources, and on the content of this congregation's marketing program.

A few congregations can mobilize the resources necessary to avoid making hard choices among attractive alternatives. For the other 99 percent of the churches, however, a useful beginning point is to identify the number-one client. Who will be assigned the most attractive meeting room? Which class will the pastor teach? How will we schedule the time on Sunday morning?

FOUR QUESTIONS

1. Can you agree on who the number-one client is for the teaching ministry in your church today? Who is number two? Who is number three?

2. Do you all agree that these should be the top three clients in that order?

3. If not, what should be the ranking of the top three clients?

4. What direction do the answers to the first three questions offer on how to expand the teaching ministry of your church?

CHAPTER SEVEN

Building in Continuity

If you ask me," declared Lynn Crandall, "the only way we are going to reach more younger adults in our Sunday school is to offer short-term classes that run for four to six weeks and cover narrowly defined topics. I don't believe it's possible to attract young adults to the old-fashioned style of Sunday school class."

"A lot of the people I know want to teach by themselves," explained Sandy McGuire. "They don't want to be part of a team. They want to be completely in charge of their own show. Besides that, we only need about a third as many teachers if we ask people to teach by themselves rather than to be part of a team. To tell you the truth, I would never sign up to be part of a teaching team. I would much prefer to carry the whole responsibility by myself."

"I'm convinced the way to attract kids today is to offer something different every week. Today's kids want to be surprised, they don't want the same old routine week after week," urged Jackie Moore. "Give them something new every week, and they'll come back the next week. Maybe we need a different teacher every week for the high school class."

"The church I grew up in had a huge adult division in the Sunday school. When I graduated from high school, I automatically went into the young adult class for people aged eighteen to twenty-nine," recalled Betsy Slama. "I left there when I was nineteen, but if I had stayed, eleven years later I would have been promoted to one of the adult classes for people aged thirty to thirty-nine. There were two classes for that age group. One was for couples and one for singles. The singles included the never-married, the divorced, and the widowed. I'm glad I left. I don't think I could have put up with that system of classifying people by age and marital status."

This discussion appears to be directed at how to organize the Sunday school in general and more particularly on how to attract more participants. These are both important topics. This conversation also introduces one of the most widely neglected of factors that should be included in any strategy to expand the teaching ministry of your church. That factor is continuity, stability, and predictability.

THE NEED FOR STABILITY ZONES

This point was explained in exceptionally lucid terms back in 1970 by Alvin Toffler in his book, *Future Shock*. In a section titled "Strategies for Survival," Toffler introduced the concept of personal stability zones.[1] A personal stability zone provides continuity, stability, predictability, enduring relationships, and a link between yesterday and tomorrow. For many mature adults the number-one personal stability zone is living with the same spouse for several decades. For others it is living in the same house and sleeping in the same bed in the same room for more than a quarter of a century. For well over one-third of all adult Americans it is living in the same community with the same friends, neighbors, and kinfolk decade after decade. For many the number-one stability zone is their church. For others it is a Sunday school class.

Children feel the need for a personal stability zone. This comes out when Dad comes home and announces that the company is transferring him to another state. A common response of the children is to resent the idea of leaving their friends. A majority of children experience great ambivalence when the time comes to graduate from elementary school and go off to middle school or junior high. In order to maintain their personal stability zone, many high school graduates take a job near home or commute to college. Perhaps the greatest disruption to a child's personal stability zone occurs when the parents announce they are separating.

At the other end of the age spectrum the aging widow resists the well-intentioned efforts of her children when they encourage her to sell the house she has lived in for forty years and enter a retirement home. A parallel is when the new minister turns out to be a dull preacher, an inept teacher, an incompetent administrator, and a lazy pastor. Many people leave to seek a new church home, but often a majority will stay, partly out of institutional loyalty and partly because this congregation continues to be their number-one personal stability zone.

CHANGE VERSUS STABILITY

A recognition of the need for personal stability zones is useful in coping with the typical negative responses to proposals for change. The first step is to affirm people's need for personal stability zones. A second ingredient in a strategy for planned change is persistence and a refusal to accept that initial rejection as final. A third is to formulate any proposal for change in a manner that minimizes the number of personal stability zones that will be threatened. A fourth is to conceptualize every proposed change as one component of a larger design that reinforces several threads of continuity. Two examples can be used to illustrate this.

One proposal originated with a study of space needs for the Sunday school. This study revealed that a Ladies' Class organized in 1942 with sixty members was still meeting in that same big second floor room. A dozen framed photographs on the wall pictured the members of this class in 1945 and several succeeding years. These photographs also revealed that the size of the class had shrunk from a peak of seventy in 1944 to fifty in 1955 to nine two years ago. The recommendation was to merge that group into a larger class of older women that met on the first floor, store those photographs in the attic, replace the teacher with the person teaching the larger downstairs class, and divide that huge second floor room into two smaller classrooms. The only point of continuity was in the five mature women who accepted this recommendation and joined what was to them a new class in a new and unfamiliar room with a new teacher and new classmates.

In another community that same week a different congregation met for the first time in their new church home. Their old building had been purchased by the city as part of an urban redevelopment program and soon would be razed. The new building had been completed a week earlier and was located a mile away. After gathering for the last time for the corporate worship of God in that beloved old building, the members marched down the street with a police escort to their new church home. Everyone carried a piece of the continuity linking the old and the new. Several carried hymnals, others carried candlesticks, banners, framed photographs, crosses, a copy of the original charter, Bibles, and other items. While they marched, three trucks moved the chancel furnishings and other furniture from the old to the new. As part of the construction program, five of the stained-glass windows had been removed and installed in the new building. The following Sunday morning the Sunday school classes met in their new rooms in the new building, but with the same classmates, the same teachers, the same hymnals, much of the same furniture, and many of the old photographs, plaques, and paintings on the walls.

The radical change of abandoning that sacred meeting place for a new church home had been tempered with dozens of threads of continuity. For many people, the favorite thread of continuity was that the pastor who had led the congregation through this change continued to serve that congregation in its new meeting place for another nine years.

EXPANSION + STABILITY = SUPPORT

The moral of these two illustrations is obvious. When you plan changes in order to expand, strengthen, and reinforce the teaching ministry of your church, reinforce continuity. Do not overload the system by making too many changes at once.

What are the points of continuity and stability? That list is endless, but among the most common suggestions on how to reinforce continuity are these five.

1. Enduring interpersonal relationships rank at the top for many people. The disruption resulting from disturbing these long-term relationships can be seen when (a) that first "baby" leaves home to go to college a thousand miles away, (b) the fourteen-year-old discovers his or her parents are seeking a divorce, (c) the beloved pastor of thirty-one years unexpectedly resigns or dies, (d) the person who taught this adult Sunday school class for twenty-three years moves away, (e) the youngest child is married, (f) this woman's hairdresser for nineteen years retires, (g) well over one-half of the members of this adult class leave because they are disenchanted with the new minister, and (h) the recently widowed man who, with his wife, was a charter member of this adult class back in 1957 appears one Sunday morning with his new wife, who is twenty years his junior.

One of the most effective means of reinforcing interpersonal relationships is shared experiences. These include the Friday evening social gatherings by adult classes every month, the visits by the parents to their son or daughter who chose a college a thousand miles away, the honeymoon for newlyweds, implementing widely shared goals as when the high school class raises the money to buy new robes for the adult choir, the weekly Thursday evening meeting of the three adults who team-teach the fifth and sixth grade class, and the weekend canoe trip for the second year confirmands.

As another example, instead of promoting the first grade Sunday school class to the second grade room, keep them in the same room with the same team of teachers and change the sign on the door.[2]

Instead of dividing that growing young adult class by an age line, organize a new young adult class and encourage those who want to help pioneer a new class to choose that option.

Instead of enlisting teachers to teach one class for one year at a time, create a three- to five-person teaching team. Build the continuity into the team, not in the individual. Thus when one teacher leaves the team, that person is replaced, but the team continues.

Instead of trying to create a post-high Sunday school class, organize a class that includes high school seniors plus those one or two years older. Many of these people were friends in school when the present seniors were sophomores. Graduating from high school is a severe break in the continuity of interpersonal relationships. Do not deepen it by making them find a new class. Mix the continuity of one more year in high school with the discontinuity of moving into a new Sunday school class in a new room with a new teacher.

Finally, plan long terms in office for leaders who represent continuity, stability, dependability, and predictability. These may include the Sunday school superintendent, class leaders, teachers, and committee members. Rotation in office is a common response to a fear of power, but it can be an enemy of continuity.

2. For many people a powerful point of continuity is meeting in the same place. Therefore, minimize the occasions when you ask a class to leave its sacred place and move to a strange meeting room.

This generalization also includes scheduling the regular meetings of the Christian education committee in the same room month after month.

3. For many people a powerful stability zone is the relationship with the same leader or pastor or teacher.

As mentioned earlier, one means of reinforcing this is to maintain the teacher-student relationship for at least three or four years. Another is to make teaching the most prestigious volunteer role in the church.

4. One of the most powerful forces for reinforcing continuity is music. Congregational singing and the anthem provide part of the continuity in corporate worship week after week. The parallel is the adult class that begins with a hymn every Sunday morning or the children's class that learns a new hymn every month or the special hymn that was composed for a particular class and is sung on a dozen occasions every year to reinforce the feeling of continuity.

5. For decades the Sunday schools used banners, pins, awards, and other forms of recognition to encourage attendance, reward excellence, inspire competition, stimulate interest, and support the vigor of that movement. These also can be some of the threads of continuity.

The simplest illustration of this is the pin that identifies one as a member of a particular class or as a graduate of an intensive Bible study program in that church. Another is the distinctive name tag created for each class, choir, or group. A third is the series of awards earned by a particular class for attendance. What do you do to reinforce the sense of belonging by people to any one component of your teaching ministry? Is it a T-shirt for every child in the Vacation Bible School? A pin or ring for every young person completing the two-year confirmation program? A membership pin for every new member on completion of that thirty-six-week course? A certificate of excellence for teachers who have completed in-service training programs? Or do you doubt that symbols, pins, and awards reinforce a sense of belonging and continuity?

In more general terms, what value do you place on continuity as you plan to change, revitalize, and expand the teaching ministry of your church?

CHAPTER EIGHT

Function, Theme, or Organization?

When we design a building for a congregation such as this one, we begin by thinking of the functions to be housed in that structure," explained the architect to the planning committee at Grace Church. "From what you've told me so far, you need space for three functions: worship, Christian education, and fellowship. In addition, we have roughed in the space you will need for offices, corridors, restrooms, and storage. The total comes to slightly over 28,000 square feet."

"A long time ago I decided I did not want to try to compartmentalize our teaching ministry in one department called Christian education," explained the recently arrived senior minister to the Personnel Committee. The discussion was over alternatives for replacing the Director of Christian Education, who was about to retire after twenty-three years of faithful service. "Instead of replacing her with a new DCE," urged this new senior minister, "I suggest we think of the teaching ministry as a theme that cuts across every facet of our life together as a worshiping community."

"I've become convinced that we made a mistake years ago when we tried to organize an evangelism committee in every congregation," continued this senior minister. "We cannot and should not try to compartmentalize evangelism. Evangelism should be a part of the ministry of every committee, board, class, program, event, and group in the church, from the choir to the trustees. Likewise, we should not try to compartmentalize the teaching ministry and delegate it to one committee and one staff person. I believe we should reconceptualize how we look at our teaching ministry and make it a major theme of our total program, rather than see it as a separate department."

"I've been studying the history of the Sunday school," commented a veteran leader at Bethany Church, "and it seems to me it reached its peak in vitality, outreach, support, and effectiveness when it was a movement owned and operated by the laity, not the professionals. In 1832, for example, a little over 40,000 people of Sunday school age were living in Philadelphia, and 28 percent of them were enrolled in a Sunday school affiliated with the American Sunday School Union. Likewise, the women's organizations in the churches were the strongest when they were owned and operated by laywomen as missionary movements. I can remember, when I was growing up in a small rural church, the Sunday school was a powerful organization, and the Sunday school superintendent was a far more influential leader than the preacher. I think we ought to go back and try to rebuild the Sunday school as a lay-owned and lay-operated institution. Professionalism has nearly killed it. Let's get back to the distinctive place of the Sunday school."

These three comments describe three radically different concepts of the teaching ministry. The architect sees it as a function of the church that requires adequate space designed for that distinctive purpose.

The senior minister views the teaching ministry as a thread or theme that permeates every facet of the life and ministry of the congregation. This is a new concept to the members of that personnel committee who continue to think in terms of functions, tasks, job descriptions, staff, budgets, salaries, space, and volunteers.

The veteran leader remembers when thousands of congregations were built around four or five lay-owned and lay-led self-winding organizations that required little from the paid staff. As rivals for the top of that list in terms of vitality, clarity of purpose, goal orientation, enthusiasm, and performance were the women's organization and the Sunday school.[1] Lower on that list of influential organizations were the men's fellowship, the chancel choir, and the youth program. When all five were at their peak, that congregation might average over five hundred at worship and be served by one pastor with a part-time secretary and a part-time custodian.

These lay-owned and lay-led movements provided continuity, a powerful lobby for that cause, enthusiastic and committed volunteers, financial resources, inspiring leadership, momentum, and vision.

WHAT IS THE QUESTION?

The question is not which approach should you follow. The crucial question is which approach are you following. Is it consistent with the role the Lord has called your congregation to fill, with your goals, and your plans?

If you have chosen the functional view of Christian education, among your top priorities will be organizing an effective committee on Christian education chaired by a competent and dedicated person, an excellent superintendent of the Sunday school, task forces or subcommittees to initiate and implement specialized educational programming, an adequate budget, attractive classrooms, and other resources necessary to fulfill your responsibilities.

If you conceptualize the teaching ministry as a theme that runs through every facet of congregational life, you first of all need a pastor who agrees with and enthusiastically supports that concept. Next you will want to make learning one of the central organizing principles for the youth ministry, add a fifteen- to thirty-minute study period to the beginning of every meeting of the governing board and all committees, expand the period for worship to allow for a thirty- to fifty-minute sermon, find a choir director or minister of music who excels as a teacher, replace the person in charge of the bulletin boards in the corridors who sees these as channels for information with a person who understands that walls do teach, change the Sunday school from classrooms to learning centers, and encourage every group, committee, task force, staff member, board, class, circle, choir, and cell to make every gathering a learning experience.

If you decide to conceptualize education as a movement[2] or organization in your congregation, you need what every social or political movement requires. That begins with one person who is convinced that this is the most important cause in the world today, committed allies, a vision of a new and better tomorrow, a minimum of organizational structure, the freedom to unilaterally mobilize resources, including volunteers and money, tenacity, enemies, persistence, and a target audience. Eventually this will evolve into a powerful organization.

In summary, one of the ways to expand the teaching ministry of your church is to be clear on how you conceptualize this in relationship to the total life of that worshiping community and to work out a strategy or an action plan that is consistent with that conceptual framework.

CHAPTER NINE

Fifteen Questions for the Sunday School

For most Protestant congregations today the Sunday school is the heart of the formal and officially organized teaching ministry of that church. For the first two centuries of Protestant church history on the North American continent, however, the sermon was the heart of the teaching ministry.[1] That pattern continued into the twentieth century in thousands of churches, but during the last half of the nineteenth century, the Sunday school began to replace the sermon as the heart of the teaching ministry. One reflection of this trend is the growing number of congregations that (a) ask the children to leave the nave to go to their Sunday school classroom during the hymn preceding the sermon, or (b) schedule Sunday school for children concurrently with the preaching service, or (c) expect the minister to spend far more time teaching than preaching.

As was pointed out earlier, a tiny proportion of pastors continue to insist that the sermon is the hub of the teaching ministry. A disproportionately large number of these pastors are senior ministers of large and rapidly growing churches. One example of this preference can be seen in the schedule that calls for the preacher to lead a Sunday school class following worship. The "lesson" is a discussion of that morning's sermon. A parallel example is the Tuesday evening study group led by the pastor that reviews and discusses last Sunday's sermon. Another example of this priority on the proclamation of God's word is the thirty- to sixty-minute sermon. In scores of smaller congregations the pastor leads a Tuesday evening group that studies, reflects on, and discusses the text for what will be next Sunday's sermon. A far larger number of preachers, however, prefer to conduct that type of study activity with peers who are pastors of other churches rather than with members. That raises the question discussed in chapter 6 about who is the client for the church's teaching ministry. The members? The pastor? Other clergy?

WHAT IS THE ROLE?

This introduces what must be one of the central questions to be discussed if the goal is to revitalize, strengthen, and expand the Sunday school. What is the place of the Sunday school in the total teaching ministry of your congregation? Is it the central component? Does it supplement the teaching done in the sermon? Does it stand alone as a lay-owned and lay-led organization in which volunteer leaders make most or all of the policy decisions? Or is it conceptualized as simply one component of a much larger system of Christian education in which paid staff are the most influential policymakers?

The discussion in this chapter rests on two assumptions that do not apply to every congregation. First, it is assumed here that the Sunday school is the principal organized component of the teaching ministry in your congregation. Second, it is assumed here that the decision has been made to begin the process of expanding the teaching ministry in your congregation by strengthening, revitalizing, and enlarging the Sunday school. Those two assumptions do not fit, nor are they appropriate for every church, but both are part of the context for this discussion.

Therefore the first step in expanding your teaching ministry is to focus on improving the Sunday school.

ALL OR PART?

The second step is to decide whether the Sunday school will be designed to offer learning opportunities to every slice of the population or only to a minority. In some congregations the majority of the adults engaged in structured educational experiences meet in classes and groups scheduled for a time other than Sunday morning. In hundreds of congregations few or no opportunities are offered for older youth or for adults to be engaged in continuing, serious, and structured Bible study. Members seeking that usually find it in a program offered by a parachurch organization rather than in their own congregation. The Sunday schools in these churches are populated largely by children, a minority of all available teenagers, and a handful of adult teachers.

A growing number of churches scatter most of their serious and in-depth Bible study classes through the week. A women's Bible study group meets on Thursday afternoon. The men's Bible class meets early Saturday morning. A two-year highly structured adult Bible study program is offered on Tuesday evenings for both men and women. The high school youth meet for Bible study on Sunday evening, and a variety of short-term classes and mutual support groups are offered during the week. The Sunday school may account for far less than one-half of all participants in the teaching ministry in a typical week.

If most of the adults involved in structured study are meeting at a time other than Sunday morning, it may be difficult to make the Sunday school the top priority in the allocation of scarce resources, and you may decide to skip this chapter.

WHY?

The third step, which has been referred to earlier, is to agree on goals, priorities, outcomes, and motivations. One group of American historians contends that fear—the fear of immigration, of urbanization, and of social disorder—was a prime motivating factor behind the Sunday school movement and other reform efforts back in the eighteenth and nineteenth centuries. Others argue that the leaders of the Sunday school movement were motivated by their drive to save souls, improve lives, overcome ignorance, reduce poverty, and other altruistic goals.[2]

For many adults the goal was and is to transmit from their heads and hearts to the heads and hearts of the next generation a mass of facts, values, beliefs, loyalties, doctrines, and data that will lead these children to commit their lives to Jesus Christ. For at least a few parents the motivation for sending their children to Sunday school is easy to explain, "It'll be good for them. It can't hurt, and it may help."

For others the answer is equally simple, "Every church needs a Sunday school."

A significant number of teachers are convinced that one of the primary goals of Sunday school is to enable children to experience the love of God that is reflected by the love of that teacher for these children. It is difficult to overemphasize how this can transform the lives of children who have never been loved by any human being. An overlapping group of leaders in the Sunday school is convinced that attitudes and values rank up there with facts and beliefs in the curriculum to be transmitted from one generation to another.

Scores of other goals and motivations could be identified for illustrative purposes, including those found in the Jerusalem Class described in chapter 2. The central question, however, remains, What do you want to happen in and through your Sunday school?

After agreement has been reached on those first three questions of (1) is the Sunday school the place to begin to expand the teaching ministry of your church, (2) will the Sunday school seek to serve everyone or only part of the population, and (3) what do we want to accomplish in and through the Sunday school, it is appropriate to look at a dozen other questions.

WHAT ARE YOUR CENTRAL ORGANIZING PRINCIPLES?

Perhaps the most subjective and the most difficult of these questions can be summarized very simply. Why will people come? What is the central organizing principle that brings people back Sunday morning after Sunday morning? What are the organizing principles that will be utilized to bring people together and make that a creative, rewarding, and meaningful learning experience?

A review of the history of the Sunday school reveals scores of motivating principles that have been used in the past two hundred years. That list includes (1) a love of God and a desire to study God's word, (2) a fear of hell and damnation, (3) a desire to grow in the faith, (4) the attractiveness of a particular teacher, (5) peer group pressures, (6) parental pressures, (7) the opportunity to meet and make new friends, (8) the chance to get out of the house to be with friends, (9) the requirement that Sunday school attendance is a prerequisite for church membership, (10) rewards and satisfactions, (11) the joy of learning, (12) the attractiveness of a particular subject to be studied, (13) the desire for self-expression and self-improvement, (14) an opportunity to learn to read and write, (15) loyalty to that congregation, (16) a sense of obligation, (17) loyalty to that denomination, (18) the promise of the opportunity to gain assistance in one's personal religious journey, (19) a means of pleasing one's spouse, (20) the desire to be a member of a loving, supportive, and caring fellowship, (21) the challenge to help pioneer a new class, (22) the opportunity to improve one's leadership skills, (23) a non-threatening opportunity to investigate the Christian faith without making a prior commitment to it, (24) a part of the courtship ritual involving a young woman who is a member and a man who is not a member of that congregation, (25) the chance for this adult male who lives and works in a world that he feels is dominated by women to be in an all-male enclave by joining that men's class, and (26) the opportunity for women who feel this is a male-dominated world to enjoy the warmth and support of an all-female class.

This is far from a complete list, but it does illustrate the point. Why will people who are not now a part of it come to your Sunday school?

THE POWER OF REDUNDANCY

The only safe answer to that question is that no one reason or motivation or attraction will work with everyone. The sensible response to that question is to build in several reasons to motivate people to return next Sunday.

A common example of this is the organization of a new adult class in the Sunday school. How can we increase the chances for success for this new venture?[3] The answer is to build in a redundant set of reasons to encourage people to come and to return. At the top of that list is an attractive and skilled teacher who can be expected to continue as the teacher for at least three years. Other factors include (1) attractive subject matter and the promise of a rewarding learning experience, (2) three or four committed officers who will serve as responsible leaders, (3) at least eight or nine social gatherings a year to strengthen the fellowship ties, (4) provisions for newcomers to meet and make friends from within that class, (5) a time for intercessory prayer every Sunday morning, (6) a class project that requires the cooperative support of all the members, (7) an attractive and comfortable meeting room that becomes the "third place" for those who seek that third place beyond home and work,[4] (8) refreshments before or after the Sunday school hour to encourage fellowship, (9) a sensitive leader who "looks after the folks" in a supportive manner—frequently this is an unofficial role filled by a self-appointed, respected, older adult in the class, (10) the active support of one staff person who rarely will be present on Sunday morning, (11) enthusiastic singing led by a personable song leader, and (12) the challenge to grow old together with friends who share similar experiences and adhere to the same value system.

Why do eight- and nine-year-old children come to that third- and fourth-grade Sunday school class week after week? Most of the regulars come for a mixture of several reasons drawn from this list: (1) parental support, (2) the attractiveness of the teachers, (3) an opportunity to express their creativity, (4) the chance to be with friends, (5) refreshments, (6) habit, (7) sibling support, (8) the joy of learning something new (for some children memorizing Bible verses produces real satisfaction and a sense of accomplishment), (9) to avoid the alternative of attending relationship, (10) the satisfactions of a structured learning experience, (11) a sense of Christian commitment, (12) to learn more about God, Jesus, and the Bible, (13) a sense of loyalty to and support for that church, (14) a change of pace in their life, (15) music, (16) the responsibility for this Sunday's assignment and (17) rewards and recognition.

The regular attenders will identify with six to ten of these reasons to explain their attendance. The irregular attenders will find that only one or two or three of those reasons have meaning for them.

How much redundancy are you building into your Sunday school?

WHAT ARE THE CHOICES?

The chaplains of the United States Navy are wondering how to attract a larger proportion of the sailors born after 1968 to Sunday morning worship. University teachers are troubled by the casual attitude this generation born after 1968 displays toward higher education. More and more churches are reporting how difficult it is to interest high school and post-high school young adults in Sunday school.

How are the churches responding to this new and radically different generation of young adults? Among the most common responses are these: (1) concentrate on the 30 percent who resemble their grandparents and offer the traditional high school Sunday school class, (2) search for the teacher(s) with the magnetic personality who can attract a wide range of youth, (3) hire someone to worry about this and delegate the responsibility to that staff member, (4) do not offer any classes for high school or post-high school age people and encourage those who do appear to participate in an adult class or to help teach in the children's division, (5) undertake a cooperative approach with one or two or three other congregations, or (6) offer a choice of three or four or five or six different classes in the Sunday school for this generation.

In more specific terms, what choices should your Sunday school offer to teenagers and young adults born since 1967 or 1968? Obviously no one response will fit all congregations, but the possibilities are limited only by one's creativity. Current examples include (1) the Sunday morning class that spends three to six months on one book of the Bible; (2) the group that stages a religious drama twice a year; (3) the class that designs, writes, and teaches the thirteen-week set of lessons to be studied by an adult class; (4) the group that acts out the faith during the week, and Sunday morning is spent reflecting on the biblical context for those weekday ministries, such as tutoring, volunteering in a nursing home, serving as a police cadet, helping to staff an after-school childcare program, working in a prison ministry, helping in a food pantry, serving in a peer counseling program, and so on; (5) the Tuesday evening study group that is engaged in an indepth study of the Scriptures; (6) playing in an intergenerational Sunday school orchestra; (7) volunteering for that elite youth cadre that is committed to changing the values of the local youth culture; (8) serving as a teacher's aide in that church's Wednesday evening teaching ministry with younger children; (9) participating in an all-male or all-female high school class, (10) making videotapes of the life and ministry of that congregation, to be shown at the annual meeting and to shut-ins; (11) helping to pioneer that new class for seventeen-, eighteen-, and nineteen-year-old youth; and (12) the action-reflection class committed to social ministries.

A central facet to this approach is to recognize that members of this generation are more likely to choose their friends on the basis of common interests than on the traditional criteria of age and grade. The larger the local high school, the less likely age and grade will be powerful factors in building friendships.

How any one congregation goes about this process of offering choices will be influenced by many factors, including (1) size, (2) physical facilities, (3) nationality or race or ethnic background of the members, (4) local traditions, (5) preferences of the pastor, (6) age of the volunteer leaders, (7) denominational traditions and policies, (8) schedules, (9) values, (10) priorities, (11) the role of creative adults in planning the program, and (12) the degree of openness and receptivity to new ideas.

The point of this illustration is not to examine how the churches will seek to meet the religious needs of the people born after 1968. That is a vast and complex subject that could be a book in itself. The point is that this generation, more than any previous generation, has forced our society to recognize the need for alternatives. Universal prescriptions to fit everyone have not been effective for many years. The generation born in the 1942–55 era demanded an unprecedented range of choices and transformed our social and political systems. This younger generation is far less demanding; they simply ignore that which does not interest them.

Most long-established congregations have two alternative courses of action. One is to continue with the two traditional choices of "take it or leave it"— and grow older and smaller. The second is to build in choices as part of a larger strategy of growing younger and larger.

A persuasive argument can be made that, for most long-established congregations, the beginning point for offering a broader range of choices to people is in the Sunday school. Among the many reasons for that dramatic decline in Sunday school attendance during the past thirty-five years in a score of the larger Protestant denominations in the United States, four surface repeatedly. The first, of course, is that the Sunday school ceased to be a high priority among denominational leaders, pastors, seminary teachers, and the laity. A second is that in the 1950s parachurch organizations began to fill the resulting vacuum with a rapidly growing variety of learning experiences directed at individuals. A third is that our society began to teach people they could expect a broad range of choices whether it was a course of study in high school, the purchase of an automobile, clothing, places to eat, housing, occupations, travel, entertainment, magazines, frames for eyeglasses, breakfast cereals, hotel and motel accommodations, or health care. Instead of eating what was placed before them or going hungry, people began to believe they were entitled to choose from among a range of attractive choices. Few Sunday schools adapted to this new world. A fourth factor was that television radically changed people's expectations about communication, public discourse, and how one learns.

If you plan to revitalize, strengthen, and expand your Sunday school, the question of how, not if, you offer people a broader range of attractive choices should be high on your agenda.

WHO ARE YOUR TEACHERS?

"In April I began my search for qualified and dedicated teachers who will commit themselves to the new Sunday school year we begin on the first Sunday of September," observed one Sunday school superintendent. "By early July I'm looking for people willing to teach for at least three or four months, and by late August I'm looking for warm bodies I can put in classrooms."

One of the crucial questions that surfaces repeatedly concerns the place of the Sunday school teachers in that network of volunteers. An examination of the system for the enlistment, placement, in-service training, and support of volunteers usually reveals the priorities of that congregation. Two examples of this were described in chapter 4. In the first, the congregation is organized around administration. This usually means the top priority in the placement of volunteers is to fill administrative positions such as trustees, the finance committee, and membership on the governing board. In the second example the congregation is organized around word and sacrament, ministry, and teaching. This creates the opportunity for making the selection of teachers a top priority.

Which is the most prestigious position in your church? President of the congregation or teaching the third- and fourth-grade Sunday school class? Church treasurer or teaching first- and second-graders? Chairing the governing board or teaching a class of high school youth? Which position would a visitor to your annual meeting rank as near the top of the status ladder among your people? Which will have the greatest impact on the lives of tomorrow's adults?

A second facet of this question about teachers may arouse the ire of those who contend that the number-one goal should be egalitarianism. One beginning point for this discussion is the assumption that this is still far from an egalitarian world and that "men's work" often commands more respect than is evoked by "women's work." In at least a few churches one example of this is that women teach in the children's division of the Sunday school and men constitute the majority of the trustees and the finance committee. Another assumption is that the Sunday school thrived back when widely respected, deeply committed, and highly influential laymen made this their top priority as volunteers in the church. This is not to suggest they did all the work. They did not! Tens of thousands of deeply committed women also staffed the Sunday school movement of the nineteenth and early twentieth centuries.

Somewhere near the middle of this century, however, two patterns began to emerge. In the theologically more liberal churches, Sunday school gradually evolved as "women's work" and enrollment declined. In the theologically more conservative churches, men continued to fill important roles in the Sunday school, and the numbers usually either grew or plateaued.

While this is not offered as a magic cure, one component of a larger strategy to strengthen the place of the Sunday school in your church could include these three steps. First, persuade two or three or four of the most widely respected and influential males in your congregation to make teaching in the Sunday school their top volunteer activity. Second, persuade two or three or four other widely respected and influential male leaders to make service on your Christian education committee their top priority for the next three years. Third, concentrate on adult males in enlisting teachers for your kindergarten, first, and second grade classes. (Incidentally, this third step is guaranteed to produce a positive response from single-parent mothers who seek a church that offers good adult male role models for their children.)

LEADERSHIP DEVELOPMENT

"I spend five days of my life every week as a teacher," replied the public school teacher who was being asked to volunteer in Sunday school. "On Sunday I want to come to Sunday school to be challenged, to grow in my faith as a Christian, to learn, to be with other adults, and to enjoy my role as a student, not to spend another day as a teacher."

"I would be glad to, but I don't know the first thing about teaching," replied a loyal and faithful member to the same request. "Put me in a room with a bunch of fifth and sixth graders, and I wouldn't even know where to begin."

Those represent two of the more common responses received by the persons who are trying to enlist teachers. These two responses also lift up the differences between two contrasting approaches to revitalizing, strengthening, and expanding the Sunday school. The more common is expressed by the wish, "I hope we're able to enlist some really good teachers for this coming year." The second reflects one of the central findings of nearly every study of the Sunday school.[5] Good teachers are most likely to be found in high commitment churches that have a carefully designed leadership development program.

From a purely pragmatic perspective, this is a key to expanding that list of potential teachers. Of greater long-term significance, however, is that a good teacher training program is far more influential than the choice of curriculum materials in determining what happens in that classroom. It also is a valuable component of that larger support system for your teachers.

Two of the central goals of every good leadership development program are (1) improving competence and (2) enhancing self-confidence. One focal point is to enable the participants to improve their competence as leaders and teachers. A second is to help raise the level of self-confidence among the participants. For most people these are mutually reinforcing goals.

What are your plans for strengthening leadership development and teacher training in your Sunday school?

THE RESOURCE CENTER

Perhaps the most overrated comment of the leadership development program often is identified by this hope: "If we can fill our library with good books and other resources, our teachers will have a place to turn for help."

That is a passive response to a need in an active world filled with increasing competition for people's attention and time. In addition, in many church buildings the library is located in an out-of-the-way room or up on the second floor or is unlocked for only a few hours each week.

Five examples will illustrate a more aggressive approach to the utilization of resources. In one church the books, magazines, videotapes, audiotapes, and other resources now are displayed in shelves that line the walls of the most heavily traveled corridor in the building. One result is what some librarians would consider an unsatisfactorily high loss through "shrinkage" as people take resources without checking them out. Most are returned. A few are not. A second result is the volume of use has tripled since these resources were moved from the second-floor room to the first-floor corridor.

Another congregation has a resource telephone number that activates a taped message. This is similar to the more widely used Dial-A-Prayer. Every week new messages are recorded for each day. Monday's is a three-minute review of a new book. Tuesday's is a three-minute introduction to one of the audio tapes or videotapes. Wednesday's is a three-minute introduction to next Sunday's lesson by a teacher from the third- and fourth-grade class. Thursday's is a three-minute lesson on teaching by the Sunday school superintendent. Friday's is a three-minute Bible story by a teacher from the first- and second-grade class. Saturday's is a promotional "Be sure to come to Sunday school tomorrow morning" message from one of the men teaching in the kindergarten class. Sunday's message is from the pastor and varies greatly from week to week in content.

A third congregation projects a clear expectation that each teacher will either read one book or view one videotape every quarter that is selected to improve that teacher's competence in the classroom. In this church the pastor selects and delivers that book or tape in quarterly pastoral calls on every teacher.

A fourth example may be the most common. The monthly meeting that brings together all teachers plus the Christian education committee always meets in the resource room and spends approximately a half hour looking at filmstrips, tapes, books, magazines, and films that fit the current schedule and needs.

A less common use of the resource room is in those churches that require one year of structured study and training by anyone who agrees to serve as a teacher in the Sunday school. In a few congregations this can be concurrent with teaching, while in others it is a requirement before beginning to teach.

How do you encourage greater use of the resources you have gathered to help your teachers? [6]

CAN YOU SHARE A STAFF PERSON?

"We're too small to be able to afford even a half-time director of Christian education, and our pastor doesn't seem interested in strengthening our Sunday school. In fact, if you ask me, I sometimes think our pastor sees the Sunday school as a threat or a rival rather than as an ally. What can we do?"

One answer is to wait and hope and pray the next pastor will be more supportive. Another is to fill the gap with volunteer leadership. A third is to share the gifts, creativity, support, skills, experience, enthusiasm, and wisdom of a full-time professional with five to eight other congregations. This has several advantages. Perhaps the most significant in the long run is that it minimizes the risk of dependency that often accompanies employment of a full-time or half-time staff person who frequently evolves into a paid superintendent of the Sunday school. A second obvious advantage is that the financial burden on any one congregation is greatly reduced. The third benefit is the assistance the professional can offer to that volunteer staff. A fourth is the staff person can become a carrier of ideas that worked in one small congregation and can be adapted to another. A fifth is simply the value of the outside third party who often can help any group of people to improve their perspective, to examine and utilize their strengths, resources, and assets, and to focus on shaping tomorrow rather than on longing for yesterday to repeat itself. A sixth is that this system can enable each congregation to benefit from a range of books, video-tapes, films, audio tapes, and similar resources that no one church could afford.

Experience suggests that geographical proximity and denominational affiliation should rank no higher than fourth or fifth on that list of criteria used to determine which congregations should cooperate in sharing the time of the same staff person. The top three variables are (1) all participating congregations should share a similar culture, (2) all participating congregations should be at or near the same point on that broad spectrum in terms of an approach to the teaching ministry, values, styles, theological stance, goals, and expectations of that shared staffer, and (3) every one of the pastors of these cooperating congregations should want to participate in this venture and also share similar expectations in regard to the assistance to be provided by this staffer. Some of the realistic observers of these cooperative efforts will rank this at the top of the list of variables that determine the eventual outcome.

Experience also suggests that this arrangement is most effective if each one of these shared resource persons (some of whom may be part-time and work with only three or four congregations) is part of a larger network that meets together at least once a month, is overseen by a full-time supervisor, and is held accountable to that network and/or the full-time supervisor.

PROJECTS AND TREASURIES?

Perhaps the most controversial of these questions concerns that ancient custom of each Sunday school class having its own treasury, treasurer, and outreach project.

In thousands of churches the call for efficiency, unity, a holistic approach to congregational life, and centralized control abolished this custom. The Jerusalem Class described in chapter 2 survived that policy decision by ignoring it. In many others, however, Sunday school classes are not permitted to have their own offerings, treasuries, treasurers, or outreach projects. All of those funds are channeled through the central treasury. What is the issue at the heart of this debate?

Some will describe the issue as simply efficiency and

economy. Why have so many treasurers, checkbooks, and bank accounts when one will suffice? Others identify the issue as accountability or control or unity or cooperation.

A better way to state the issue is more complicated. One of the most useful cohesive forces for turning a loose collection of individuals into a closely knit and unified group is for them to share in a common goal. Frequently this is expressed by raising money for a worthy outreach project. The power of this basic organizing principle is strengthened if the members not only contribute money but also give of their time, energy, creativity, and sweat to make that project a success story. Examples range from a dinner to raise money for missions, to repairing secondhand bicycles for an inner-city ministry, to a work camp mission trip on another continent, to renovating a classroom in the building.

If the new policy forbids classes to have treasuries, treasurers, and outreach projects, what will replace that as an equally powerful central organizing principle to strengthen cohesion and reinforce a sense of class loyalty? That may be the central issue in this debate.

WHAT ARE THE RALLYING POINTS?

The history of social movements is filled with examples of the fact that every movement needs a redundant set of rallying points to attract and hold the participants in that movement. The list of these rallying points is endless, but it always begins with a cause that becomes the most important agenda in the world for the leaders of that movement. That list usually also includes the magnetic leader, the highly committed volunteer workers, and the repeated occasions for people to come together to rally in support of this cause and to reinforce their sense of unity.

This pattern can be seen in the history of the Sunday school movement,[7] the labor movement, the civil rights movement, the environmental movement, the campaign inspired by Franklin D. Roosevelt called "The March of Dimes" to wipe out polio, the contemporary movements on behalf of victims of AIDS, the creation of a new religious tradition by those who have become disillusioned with the denomination of which they have been a part, as well as in a huge variety of social protest movements.

What does this say to the Sunday school? If you seek to expand your Sunday school, exploit the value of a rallying point. The obvious example, of course, is a big and carefully designed annual Rally Day to mark the beginning of the new Sunday school year. Other examples include the Sunday school picnic, the annual awards Sunday, T-shirts, Vacation Bible School (see chapter 12), pins, attendance banners, the float representing your Sunday school in the local community parade, the BIG Sunday school missions project for the year that requires everyone's support to be successful, the annual dinner to honor and thank the teachers, colorful bulletin boards, the yellow brick linoleum road that leads from the main entrance of the building to the children's department, the annual workday for renovation of the facilities, the visit from a missionary sponsored by one or more of the classes, the Sunday school orchestra, and the Sunday school softball and/or volleyball team in the local church league.

What are the rallying points you use to reinforce people's loyalty to your Sunday school?

WHO ARE YOUR COMPETITORS?

Once upon a time the family was the number-one competitor for the time, loyalty, and interest of children. Later the public schools came along to compete with the family and the churches for the time, loyalty, and interest of children. Subsequently, other competitors appeared. These include nursery schools, tax-supported kindergartens, Scouting, 4H, the YMCA and the YWCA, magazines and dime novels, the local park districts, radio, Little League, television, soccer, and, more recently, a growing variety of philanthropic, charitable, and religious organizations concerned about the health, safety, education, welfare, entertainment, recreation, and future of children. In addition, the competition has been enhanced by entrepreneurial individuals who have concluded that they can help children and also make a living by teaching children to twirl a baton, to dance, to sing, to play a musical instrument, or to become skilled gymnasts. Another group of entrepreneurs have decided they can combine doing good and making a living by inviting children or youth to a summer camp where they can improve their computer skills or lose weight or play basketball or learn to swim or improve their skills in interpersonal relationships or simply get away from home and have fun.

In hundreds of communities an introduction to the range of this competition can be found by watching the annual community parade on Memorial Day or the Fourth of July or Labor Day. Count the number of secular units in the parade that are organized to serve children. Also count the number of religious organizations in that parade that lift up a ministry with children.

A more useful approach would be to build a list of the various organizations, agencies, and firms that are competing with your Sunday school for the time, loyalty, and interest of children and youth. What is the distinctive appeal of each one? Why do children repeatedly return to participate in the activities of each of these competitors? What does that suggest about how you can make your Sunday school more attractive in this highly competitive world? Perhaps most important of all, what are these competitors not doing that needs to be done and that may be accomplished in and through your congregation?

HOW DO WE BETTER SERVE CHILDREN AND YOUTH?

What may be the supreme irony of contemporary American society can be stated in two sentences. First, Americans are investing record amounts of money, volunteer time, organizational resources, professional expertise, and governmental funds in an unprecedented variety of programs designed to help children and youth. Second, the public record suggests that the American environment is less and less conducive to the rearing of healthy, well-adjusted, competent, and responsible children and youth.

Countless volumes of research have been published in recent years that describe the problem.[8] Whether the focus of the research is on reading skills, moral conduct, ethical standards, crime rates, unwed teenage mothers, school dropout rates, SAT scores, analytical ability, citizenship, respect for other persons and their property, a mastery of American history, knowledge of the biblical narrative, the work ethic, honesty, neighbor-centered concerns, civility, physical health or preparation for eventual entry into the labor force, the findings are somewhere between disheartening and discouraging.

The research suggests something is not working. It can be useful to understand what the competitors identified in the previous section are doing, but it probably will be far more useful to discover what they are not doing.

While the response to that question must be tailored to fit your local situation, these questions can offer a beginning point.

1. Is the primary focus of the competition on the child or on the family? Perhaps your church can make a significant and unique contribution by concentrating your resources on strengthening the family?

2. Who is teaching moral values and ethical conduct? Can you do that?

3. Which of your competitors are effectively teaching reading and writing skills? Can you include the mastery of these skills in your Sunday school? (All readers born before 1900 will remember that was a central reason for the existence of the first Sunday schools.)

4. Who is helping children and youth integrate a deep personal relationship with a loving God with an active commitment to serve? [9] This was one of the accomplishments of the Sunday schools of the 1900–1925 era. Could that become the unique contribution of your Sunday school to today's children?

5. Who among your competitors is most proficient in teaching effective parenting skills? Even if you can name three or four competitors who are doing this, you may be able to offer a unique ministry by teaching parenting skills from within a Christian context.

This is not offered as an exhaustive list, but simply to illustrate three points. First, do not surrender because you feel overwhelmed by the competition and the fact that you may not be able to compete on their agendas without comparable resources. Second, build on your strengths, resources, and assets to offer a distinctively Christian ministry with children and youth. Third, study the evidence to discover where you most likely will be able to have an influential impact.

Nearly all of the research agrees on three points. First, the family usually is the most influential institution in our society for the transmission of values, social skills, attitudes, beliefs, loyalties, language skills, and other cultural norms from one generation to the next. Second, the first several years of formal education often are the second most influential force in the socializing of children into our culture. Third, parental involvement in all socializing experiences (family, school, 4H Club, Scouting, Little League, Sunday school, and so on) is crucial if the children and youth are to secure the maximum benefits from these experiences.

How can your teaching ministry in general and your Sunday school in particular build on these points of agreement? By minimizing the perception that parents are welcome to "drop the children off for Sunday school" while those parents go home to read the newspaper? By offering parenting classes? By organizing an early childhood development center that functions on a six-day (Sunday through Friday) week? By enlisting and training older siblings and parents to serve as teachers in the Sunday school? By organizing a Christian day school? By strengthening the nurturing environment of your Sunday school? By changing the focus from "ministries with children" to "ministries with families that include young children"? By replacing your youth director with a staff member trained in ministries with families that include teenagers? By welcoming home schooling families into your teaching ministry? By conceptualizing your Sunday school as "family"? By making the celebration of World Marriage Day (the second Sunday in February) a special day in your Sunday school?

WHAT ARE THE FRINGE BENEFITS?

Most people tend to look at the Sunday school as primarily an educational venture. "Well, what did you learn today?" the father asks his son as he picks him up after the fourth-grade Sunday school class.

A good Sunday school provides a range of benefits beyond Christian education. The Jerusalem Class discussed in chapter 2 illustrates this point. Likewise, one way to strengthen and expand the Sunday school is to affirm the value of these fringe benefits.

The research conducted by the Search Institute repeatedly emphasized that by "nurturing an ongoing growth in faith," congregations strengthen both denominational and congregational loyalties.[10]

Another benefit, which has a chicken-and-egg dimension to it, reflects a basic pattern. The higher the average attendance in the Sunday school, the higher the worship attendance-to-membership ratio. In part, this clearly is a reflection of the self-fulfilling expectation described in chapter 5.

Occasionally a valuable fringe benefit of a strong Sunday school surfaces following the departure of an unusually popular preacher. A common pattern in those circumstances is (a) a sharp decline in worship attendance, (b) the disappearance of many of the members who joined during that minister's tenure, and (c) scapegoating the successor for what happens.

Another pattern is that all the numbers—worship attendance, membership, contributions, Sunday school attendance—remain high following the departure of that magnetic personality. The most common explanation behind that pattern is the network of redundant ties that reinforced the loyalty of the people to that congregation as a whole, rather than to that popular preacher. These usually include an outstanding ministry of music, a large network of closely knit and unified adult classes, a widely supported commitment to worldwide missions, and a growing women's organization. That also is a great legacy to leave to a successor!

From a long-term perspective one of the most beneficial fringe benefits from a strong adult Sunday school comes when these classes are viewed as opportunities to teach churchmanship to a new generation of members, to transmit an understanding or an appreciation for that congregation's heritage and traditions, and to train future leaders.

For those ministers who value this, an important fringe benefit is the adult class taught by the pastor. One example of how this can enhance the relationship between the minister and the members requires a 65- to 75-minute period for Sunday school. Well before that period begins, people begin to arrive, go to this large meeting room for a snack and beverage, talk and wait for the class to begin. On 36 to 45 Sundays a year, the pastor teaches this class. This gives the participants a chance to see the pastor in a teaching role, to become better acquainted with their minister, and to become valued members of this congregation within that larger fellowship. This also can be an attractive alternative for those parents who do not want to be part of a "regular" class while their children are in Sunday school, it can be an easy entry point for church shoppers and other newcomers who want to enter on their own terms at their own pace, it often is an intergenerational experience, and it can offer an opportunity for the pastor to identify needs that otherwise might not be visible.

This alternative usually works best if the class includes at least 50 or 60 participants, is organized as a large group experience, focuses on Bible study, is primarily a lecture format, and meets in an easy-to-find and spacious room with comfortable chairs.

For many congregations the Sunday school can be a ministry that can (1) provide attractive entry points for future new members and for the assimilation of newcomers (see chapter 15), (2) be the best opportunity that church offers for adults to model for children the life-style of the committed Christian, (3) offer excellent opportunities for stewardship education, especially for young children, (4) be the place where adults meet their future spouse (what better place to meet your future spouse than in church?), (5) reach some of those adults who have found the traditional worship experience to be boring or irrelevant with the good news that Jesus Christ is Lord and Savior, (6) become "my family" for those who do not find the support of family at any other point in their lives, and (7) in those long-established congregations that display a high degree of diversity among the members and in the reasons why they are part of that church, adult classes can be a means of building a sense of unity in a sea of heterogeneity. Many congregations make a highly intentional effort to build a high degree of homogeneity in each new class. That is their answer to the question of how to have unity amid diversity. That remarkably heterogeneous and unified congregation often is really a combination of (a) homogeneous classes, groups, organizations, choirs, cells, and circles, (b) a strong emphasis on clearly defined and widely supported goals, and (c) intentional ministerial leadership that initiates rather than reacts.

What are the fringe benefits your Sunday school offers? How do you exploit those fringe benefits as you seek to expand your Sunday school? [11]

CHAPTER TEN

Why Have Adult Classes?

Four major contemporary trends represent part of the context for a discussion of adult classes. The most highly visible trend comes from the reports of a score of the large denominations of a drop in the number of people enrolled in their adult Sunday school classes. Far less visible, but at least equally significant, is the growing number of adults born after 1945 who are regular and active members of a Bible class or study group that meets at some time other than during the Sunday school hour. Overlapping these two trends is the third: the record number of adults enrolled in highly structured, serious, and indepth continuing Bible study groups taught by trained leaders. The fourth is the power of a high quality, high commitment adult teaching ministry in reaching and attracting people born after World War II.

In other words, the number-one pragmatic reason for offering adult classes can be stated very simply. "Instead of passively watching our congregation grow older and smaller, we want to grow younger and larger." That institutionally self-serving motivation will not satisfy the purists among those who place evangelism at the top of the church's priority list, nor will it please those who believe that outreach is a more valid motivating force than institutional survival. Likewise that motivation will not appeal to those leaders who believe people should not choose a church on the basis of their own personal and religious needs, but rather on the basis of where they are needed.

The point of this introductory discussion is not to pro-
voke a divisive debate over the relative purity of various
motives. The point is that the ecclesiastical landscape currently includes a record number of adults who are seeking a
high quality teaching ministry. For many this is far more
influential than denominational affiliation or geographical
proximity or inherited loyalties when they shop for a new
church home.

So why should your church offer adult classes? The number-one reason may be to respond to the religious needs of
some of those millions of people who have that at or near
the top of their church shopping list.

IS THIS TO BE A LEARNING COMMUNITY?

For those congregations designing a strategy to reach and
serve the generations born after 1940, adult classes may
become a central component of that strategy. One expression of this is the goal of functioning as a learning community.

A typical example of this goal is when the long-range
planning committee in the aging and shrinking congregation wrestles with the twin questions of purpose and role.[1]
Three types of congregations frequently choose the role of
learning community. One is the theologically conservative
or evangelical church that is seeking to reach the seekers,
inquirers, searchers, and pilgrims from among that slice of
people born after 1955 who are not actively involved in the
life of any worshiping community. In these churches the
twenty-five to fifty-minute sermon often is the number-one
component of the teaching ministry. The second is adult
classes.

Another is the congregation located on the liberal half of
the theological spectrum that is served by a pastor who was
reared in a theologically conservative environment and

twenty or thirty years later moved to a more liberal theological position. A common slogan is, "We are the church for the thinking adult who seeks a non-doctrinaire approach to the faith." Another is, "We won't tell you what you must believe, but we will help you on your faith journey."

A third is the congregation that acts on the assumption that a parent is a child's first and most influential teacher. These churches focus their appeal more narrowly on families with young children. Their self-identified role as a learning community often includes (1) a Sunday-through-Friday early childhood development center, (2) parenting classes, (3) an excellent nursery, (4) a high quality Sunday school for children, (5) classes designed to help parents function effectively as transmitters of the Christian faith, (6) intensive adult Bible study groups that meet for two to three hours forty to forty-five weeks a year to cover a two or three year curriculum, (7) adult classes that study theology and doctrine, (8) groups for junior high and senior high youth built around serious Bible study, (9) women's Bible study classes, and (10) men's Bible study classes. These churches can be found at any point of the theological spectrum, but the vast majority are on the high commitment half of that spectrum.

In other words, adult classes are an essential component of the church that sees itself as a learning community.

THE CONGREGATION OF CONGREGATIONS?

Four overlapping contemporary patterns provide another answer to the question of why your church might offer adult classes. The first is that the number of Protestant congregations averaging over 800 at worship has at least quadrupled since 1950. The second is that churchgoers born after 1945, if they perceive they have a choice, can be found in disproportionately large numbers in these very large congregations. The third trend is the growing number of younger adults who expect the teaching ministry will offer opportunities both to learn content and to meet and make close friends. They want function (education) and relationships (friends) in one package. Fourth, these large churches can offer a broad range of very high quality ministries and programs, but the price tag is anonymity.

The both-and solution to the either-or problem of choice and quality versus intimacy is to transform the conceptual framework. Instead of conceptualizing this as a congregation of 1,450 members, the operational assumption is that this is a congregation of congregations. The most common expression of this is that each adult class, whether it meets on Sunday morning or Tuesday evening or Saturday afternoon, is conceptualized as a small congregation. Each of these congregations has an appointed teacher, two to five elected officers, a "pastor" who is a member of the program staff, an outreach project, and, usually, a treasury. It is a "small church" that excels in expressions of neighbor-centered love, support, intercessory prayer, caring for one another, and intimacy. It provides every member with the advantage of being part of a small Christian community, but every member also has access to the total ministry and program of that large congregation. The adult classes are the building blocks for this definition of congregational life.

FIND A NEED AND MEET IT!

From the perspective of an organizational structure, the adult class provides a useful conceptual framework for those congregations that pride themselves on their sensitivity to human needs. Instead of expecting the pastor or the staff to respond to every need for pastoral care, these congregations assume that the group life will provide much of that care. (One perspective on this was offered in chapter 5 in the discussion on mutual support groups.)

These classes or groups usually come into existence in response to one narrowly defined need. One may be formed as a support group for the recently widowed. Another for the adult children who still carry the scars from that painful separation and divorce of their parents. A third may be created for those grieving over the death of a child. Another may be for those going through a traumatic divorce. Occasionally one is organized for parents of developmentally disabled children. Another may be for parents who just moved into the empty nest stage of life. A growing number of classes are for parents of adopted children born into a different racial or ethnic heritage.

Sometimes these mutual support groups function as support systems for a passing parade of wounded birds who fly away after recovery. Frequently the friendships formed are so deep the people decide to continue together as a permanent adult class.

One example of the continuing class that combines intimacy, caring, mutual support, long-term friendships, and learning studies self-help books written from a Christian perspective. Perhaps the most widespread example are the classes that study books written by authors such as M. Scott Peck. This class usually thrives if the discussion is led by an excellent teacher (often a pastoral counselor, psychiatrist, psychologist, social worker, or college teacher), schedules eight to fifteen social gatherings annually, has a class outreach project, enjoys the leadership of committed and caring officers, and, of course, enjoys refreshments before or after class.

Four of the critical components for building this approach to ministry are (1) skilled staff, (2) an organizational structure that affirms, supports, and seeks to strengthen the group life, (3) a recognition of the value of creating a new mutual support group once or twice or three times a year, depending on size and need, and (4) a congregational self-image of being a seven-day-a-week church.

THE CHURCH GROWTH STRATEGY

Advocates of evangelism and numerical growth usually affirm adult classes as an essential component of that strategy. Adult classes in the teaching ministry can be used to encourage numerical growth.

The most obvious value is as an entry point for future new members and to facilitate the assimilation of new members. (See chapter 15.) Adult classes also can facilitate that change in congregational life-style from the church that is built around a network of one-to-one relationships with the pastor at the hub of that network into one that affirms the group life.[2] Adult classes also can be a useful part of a larger strategy to encourage greater participation by adult males. (See chapter 13.) Adult classes can strengthen the political clout of the Christian education committee and the church growth task force in the allocation of scarce resources. These classes also can be a valuable component of a larger strategy to reach and serve more people by expanding the range of choices open to adults. Adult classes can undergird a church growth strategy by serving as a supplier of future volunteer leadership.

While this may arouse some debate, adult classes also can strengthen your church growth strategy by challenging that old cliche, "If you can get the children, the parents will follow." Whether that generalization ever described reality is questionable, but it clearly was made obsolete by the arrival of the private automobile and the disappearance of the geographical parish. The vast majority of numerically growing congregations report that only a tiny fraction of their new members walk to church—and few children have a driver's license. In today's world the churches that are attracting large numbers of children report that few walk, they are transported by their parents or by church buses. In brief, the most effective approach to increasing the enrollment of children in your Sunday school is to improve the attractiveness of your program to parents—and one component of that strategy can be the adult classes.

The adult class taught by the pastor also can be an exceptionally attractive entry point for pilgrims, searchers, inquirers, and seekers.[3] Finally, the adult class can be a reassuring refuge for those who "want to see our church grow" but are alarmed by that flood of strangers who begin to fill all those empty pews.

HOW DO WE REACH CHILDREN?

Strengthening and expanding the adult classes can be the best beginning point if your goal is to expand attendance in the children's division. One component of that strategy is to teach children that Sunday school is important. The most effective way of doing that is modeling. Children believe that what is important is what adults choose to do. Thus the number-one way to teach children that Sunday school is important is for them to see adults in the Sunday school classes. If children see adults participating in Sunday school and enjoying that participation, most children will want to emulate that adult behavior.

Likewise the importance of Sunday school is reinforced when children see the teachers making preparation for and teaching Sunday school a high priority in their lives. Third, children see junior high and senior high youth attending and enjoying Sunday school. Another part of this strategy is to make the position of Sunday school superintendent the most prestigious volunteer office in that church.

RAISING EXPECTATIONS

What does your church expect of people? Is your church a high-expectation and low-performance congregation? Or is it a low-expectation and low-performance congregation? What proportion of your members share in the corporate worship of God on the typical Sunday? If that figure is below 70 percent, this suggests it is a low-expectation church.

A strong adult program in your teaching ministry can be one way to raise expectations and performance. Attractive adult classes in the Sunday school can be the most effective single means of projecting the expectation that "we assume everyone will be here for two hours or more on Sunday morning." (A small percentage of members will want to be in an adult class, teach in the children's division, and also participate in worship. In larger congregations the schedule can be designed to fulfill that three-period expectation by scheduling at least one adult class concurrently with one or both of the two worship services.) This runs counter to the popular "one-hour package" that enables parents to be in worship while their children are in Sunday school. The best response to that demand is the combination of the two-hour expectation plus attractive adult classes plus the expectation that children of all ages will attend worship.

In simple terms, one way to increase worship attendance is to offer meaningful and memorable preaching. Another is excellent music. A third is to schedule adult classes that meet before worship and add them to that list of motivating forces that cause your members to get out of bed and come to church on Sunday morning.

Strengthening your teaching ministry with adults can be an effective component of a larger strategy to revitalize your ministry and to improve your capability to meet the religious needs of people.

CHAPTER ELEVEN

What Is the Role of Parents?

Among the half dozen lessons coming out of research on education in the public schools of the United States on which there is broad-based agreement, none is more significant than the influence of parents. Scores of research studies have pointed out that the number of dollars spent per student is not the key variable some had hoped it was. If expenditures per student was the critical factor, it would be relatively easy to pour more money into the schools as the decisive factor in reforming public education. The research also lifts up the role of the teacher and of the principal. These reports also point out the value of smaller classes, but that is not as crucial as many had argued. Discipline is an essential component to a good learning environment, but that too is not the most important single variable. High quality modern physical facilities also help, but again that is not the critical variable.

What is the best predictor of how a child will fare in public school? The answer, of course, is the family context in general and the parents in particular. Parents are the first and the most influential teachers a child will ever have. To be more precise, a parent's involvement in the education of a child is the best predictor of how that child will fare in school.

What can you do about this? Perhaps the most common response is to passively wish that "our parents would show a greater interest in what we're doing with their children in Sunday school." The second most common response to this question about the role of parents in your teaching ministry is to turn to parents in recruiting most of the teachers in the children's division of the Sunday school. A third, and rapidly growing, response can be seen in those churches that offer parenting classes that stress the role of the parent as the first teacher that child will encounter out in this world.

A fourth possibility was described in the previous chapter for those congregations that identify themselves as learning communities. One facet of that scenario is to prepare parents to be the primary Christian educators with their own children.

While it currently is an alternative for only about a million children (but that is quadruple the 1980 figure), a fifth response is to begin with those interested parents who are home schoolers. Rather than enroll their children in a public or private elementary school, these parents have decided to educate their children at home. The congregations that include home schoolers thus have a ready market for a teaching ministry that requires a huge investment of time, energy, commitment, and creativity by parents.

A sixth, and by far the most demanding, response to this question on the role of parents could be to adapt the Parents as Teachers (PAT) program mandated by the Missouri state legislature in 1984 for all of the 543 public school districts in that state.[1] In most congregations this approach calls for the training of several volunteers. Each volunteer will serve three to five families and make twice-a-month, one-hour-long house calls. The purpose of these calls is to help each parent become a more effective Christian educator with children. These volunteers may bring curriculum materials to be used by the parents, but the primary purpose of each call is not to bring materials. The primary purpose is to help each parent enhance his or her parenting skills in general and Christian educator skills in particular. A critical component of this approach is clarity of goals for both the volunteer visitors and the parents. These volunteers are *not* social workers; they are enablers and teachers! In larger congregations a paid staff member may be called who will build and oversee this team of volunteers.

A far more common approach can be seen in high expectation churches. Unlike those congregations that operate as voluntary associations, these high expectation churches project clearly defined goals and roles. One example is the church that requires every parent of a child in the Sunday school to come to the church and meet with that child's teacher at least four times a year. Another is the church that requires all parents to work in the children's division every Sunday morning. A few are teachers, more are teachers' aides, others serve in specialized roles such as music teacher, itinerant clown, hall monitor, receptionist, pianist, teacher-in-training, audio-visual specialist, chaperon, camcorder operator, or puppeteer. Every parent is required to work in the children's division so they can have firsthand knowledge of what is happening.

A parallel approach can be found in many Sunday-Friday early childhood development programs where every parent is required to contribute forty to eighty hours annually as a volunteer.

What is your system for enhancing the involvement of parents in your teaching ministry with children?

CHAPTER 12

What Is the Role of the Vacation Bible School?

Are your children lonesome for their friends back where you came from? Do they complain 'I'm bored' or 'We don't have anything to do'? Are you eagerly awaiting the opening of school this fall so that your children will have a chance to meet and make new friends?

"One solution to your problem is to enroll your children in our Vacation Bible School that will run from Monday through Friday the last week of July and the first week of August this year.

"During these two weeks your children will have the opportunity to meet and make new friends, to learn more about Jesus, to deepen their understanding of God's will in their lives, to come to a greater appreciation of God's creation, to learn how we Christians can express more fully our love for one another, and to learn more about what the Bible offers us."

These three paragraphs were followed by details on the schedule, how to register, the location, and a couple of sentences about the sponsoring church.

A copy of this one-page flyer was mailed in mid-July to every new family that had moved into any one of the three surrounding zip code areas during the previous two months. In late June a different flyer publicizing the upcoming Vacation Bible School had been mailed to every household in these same three zip code areas.

The congregation that does this year after year is convinced by the results that the Vacation Bible School is its best single avenue for expanding its teaching ministry. The leaders point to a half dozen ways this has been a valuable strategy.

First, of course, they use their Vacation Bible School as an attractive, non-threatening, and convenient entry point for newcomers to the community to become acquainted with that congregation. This does not require a final or irrevocable or binding commitment by those newcomers. They can test out this church on a short-term basis before deciding whether or not this will be their new church home.

Second, on both the first and second Friday evenings, the schedule calls for family gatherings. The agenda includes a chance for parents to see what their children have been doing and learning, to meet the parents of other children, as well as to get acquainted with the staff.

Third, they begin with the stranger's agenda. For many parents who are newcomers to that community, a source of frustration is that their children have left their friends behind. Many churches apparently operate on the assumption that the responsibility for helping new arrivals meet and make new friends is the responsibility of neighbors, the local park or recreation district, Scouting, the swimming pool, or the parents themselves. This approach to Vacation Bible School is designed to offer an attractive and positive response to that parental frustration. It is based on the assumption that the most effective way to build a relationship with a stranger is to begin with the stranger's agenda.

Fourth, the law of probability suggests that most of the children who are new to this community probably will find at least some of their new friends from among the children of members. This can lead to friendships between the members and the newcomers. That friendship can be the bridge that brings these newcomers into that church.

Fifth, the Vacation Bible School can be a testing ground for potential future teachers in the year-around teaching ministry. At least a few potential future teachers are reluctant to make a commitment to a ten or twelve or twenty-four-month assignment, but they will agree to teach for two weeks. Those two weeks can be the opportunity for both the fledgling teacher and the leaders in the teaching ministry to decide whether or not they want to enter into a longer relationship.

(Those who look to women *not* employed in the labor force for volunteers will be pleased to note the number of American women, age 45-64, *not* in the labor force increased from 10.8 million in 1950 to 11.2 million in 1990. The number of American women age 65 and over who are not in the labor force nearly tripled from 6.4 million in 1950 to 17 million in 1990. Many of these women feel they are too old to teach week after week in Sunday school, but will volunteer for Vacation Bible School. Men who have chosen early retirement can be another source of teachers.)

Sixth, and many will want to place this at the top of the list of benefits of a two-week Vacation Bible School, this can be an enjoyable, memorable, and enriching learning experience for everyone involved.

A growing number of churches run a variation of this program by scheduling the full two weeks for evenings and offer learning experiences for all ages. This has all six of the advantages described earlier, plus the focus is on the whole family constellation rather than on children.

At the other end of that spectrum that describes the range of approaches to Vacation Bible School is when three to eight congregations from various traditions come together to offer a three-day program for children of members. This effort can be pointed to with pride as a symbol of Christian unity, as a venture in intercongregational cooperation, and as a way to minimize the work load on any one congregation while fulfilling the obligation to "at least offer something for the children during the summer."

Another variation is the church that offers a one-week Vacation Bible School in June in order to be able to serve the children who may be on vacation later in the summer, a second one-week program in July that is designed for both newcomers and members, and a third week in August that is for all ages and meets during the evening.

As a general rule the total enrollment in Vacation Bible School, if it is an attractive and well-publicized program, can be expected to be the equivalent of somewhere between 15 and 60 percent of your reported membership.

SEVEN QUESTIONS

These comments provide the context for raising seven questions.

1. Do you offer a Vacation Bible School every summer?

2. If yes, what are the goals of that program?

3. If yes, is it conceptualized as one component of the total teaching ministry?

4. If not, why not?

5. If yes, how can you improve it as part of a larger effort to expand the teaching ministry of your church?

6. If no, could this become a beginning point for a larger strategy to expand your teaching ministry?

7. How many people do you expect will enroll in your Vacation Bible School? What will you need to do to achieve that goal?

CHAPTER THIRTEEN

Where Are the Men?

Three of the most widely used tactics for limiting the number of participants in the teaching ministry are to (1) concentrate on members and children of members, (2) focus on the needs of women and children, and (3) limit the number of men who are asked to teach and/or serve on the Christian education committee. That combination works! Literally thousands of congregations have followed those three rules with the result that three-fourths to nine-tenths of the adults involved in the teaching ministry are female.

One strategy for expanding the teaching ministry is to encourage greater participation by adult males. How can that be accomplished? That question does not have a single and simple answer. Among the many ways that are often used to increase adult male participation in the teaching ministry, these nine appear repeatedly.

Perhaps the best is to enlist only adult male volunteers to teach the kindergarten class. Women, as a group, tend to talk to five-year-olds. Men are far more likely to pick the children up, carry them around, hug them, play with them on the floor, and motivate the children to want to return next Sunday morning.

This practice also has tremendous appeal to single-parent mothers who seek good male adult role models for their children. This practice also models and affirms a role for men in the teaching ministry.

A second practice is to enlist several men to become trained specialists in teaching one section of that extended new-member orientation class described in chapter 5. One man teaches a four-week class on the Old Testament to every new-member class. Another man teaches the five-week section on the doctrines and polity of this denomination to each new-member class. This search for specialized competence in a narrowly defined field makes it easier to say, "Yes, I will teach that."

Historically, one of the two most common practices to encourage greater participation by men has been and is the all-male class. This is the closest to a guaranteed winner on this list if (a) the pastor is an excellent teacher, (b) the pastor agrees to teach this all-male class at least forty-four Sundays a year, and (c) the pastor is female. One way to keep it small is to open it to women. A second is to have a different teacher every week. A third is to meet every other week. For many men this class becomes a meaningful "third place"[1] or a dependable "stability zone."[2] That is reinforced by the predictability, the continuity, and the dependability of the culture of that class.

In many churches this all-male enclave meets for Bible study, prayer, breakfast, and fellowship every Saturday morning.

Historically, the other common practice for encouraging male participation has been to find a respected man to serve as Sunday school superintendent. In today's world that raises another issue. Which is the higher priority? Should the choice of a Sunday school superintendent symbolize egalitarianism and no barriers based on gender? Or should that selection be used to reinforce the symbolic role of men in the Sunday school? That is obviously a divisive tradeoff!

A fifth practice to encourage greater male participation that is widely used today requires all teaching teams to include at least one adult male. The first barrier to implementing this alternative, of course, is adoption of the concept of team teachers versus solo teachers. Most congregations report it is easier to enlist adults, both male and female, to serve as part of a teaching team than to recruit solo teachers. Ideally each team will include at least two male teachers so they can offer support for one another.

Very few employers today hire a man and set him to work on that new job without any on-the-job training or orientation. (Two of the big exceptions are (a) those congregations who call a new minister directly from seminary and (b) those churches that call a new associate minister who has never served in that role before.) One of the most effective means of increasing the number of male leaders and teachers is training for a specific assignment. A few denominations offer this, but too often these training programs for volunteer leaders are directed at administrative concerns rather than at teaching roles.

One of the most effective success stories is the extended training program for those who offer to lead a two or three or four year adult Bible study group. Most of these packaged programs are open to both men and women as leaders. With a little extra effort it often is possible for a majority of those volunteers to be adult males.

Back in the 1920s the typical Sunday school orchestra consisted of twelve to twenty men plus a few teenage boys. Today it is more likely that women will represent a majority of the orchestra. This still can be an attractive entry point for men, and a reasonable goal would be that at least one-half of those playing in the orchestra would be male.

Finally, any serious effort to involve more men in the teaching ministry should include a careful study of the gender differences reported in the SEARCH research project.[3] These researchers found that 40 percent of the women born back in the 1928–48 era reported "high faith maturity" compared to only 15 percent of men from that same age cohort. By contrast, 49 percent of the women and 35 percent of the men born before 1928 displayed "high faith maturity." Do those differences represent age, gender, or generation? Did the people born before 1928 grow up in an environment more favorable to and supportive of one's faith journey?

Do these comparisons suggest that the goal of attracting more men may require a different approach to programming than is used to attract more women? Does the faith journey of men differ from the faith journey of women? If so, how do you respond to those differences?

Among the several factors that help create a favorable context for effective Christian education with adults are these four: (1) the teachers display a mature and deep faith, (2) the pastor not only has a strong commitment to adult Christian education but also is actively involved in doing it and knows how to do it, (3) the program emphasizes Bible knowledge and understanding of the Bible, and (4) adults are encouraged to talk about their faith and faith questions.

What happened in the churches back in the 1930s, 1940s, and 1950s that was far more beneficial to the faith pilgrimage of women than to men?

When this is pushed one step further, what were the churches doing the first four decades of this century that provided a more positive environment for the faith journey of men than was present in churches during the next three decades?

Are these questions relevant to your goal of attracting a larger number of men as you seek to expand the teaching ministry of your church?

CHAPTER FOURTEEN

The Nursery

The thirty-three-year-old husband drove up to the main entrance at First Church where he stopped, jumped out, and went around to the right side of the car. He opened the rear door and unstrapped the nine-month-old baby from the safety seat in the rear. As he handed that precious bundle to his wife, he promised, "Wait right here, and I'll be back as soon as I park the car."

A few minutes later this couple, who were first-time visitors to First Church, had found their way to the second floor nursery. "This isn't for us," whispered the wife as she pointed to the sign above the door which read, "Infants Through Age Three." "Let's check it out," he whispered back. As they walked into the room, a thirteen-year-old girl came over and offered, "Here, I'll take your baby."

"Who's in charge here?" asked the mother as she displayed no sign of surrendering her baby to this young teenager.

"Mrs. Baxter is in charge, but she hasn't arrived yet. Shelley and I help out here," explained the teenager as she pointed to another girl who appeared to be about thirteen or fourteen years old. "Sometimes Mrs. Baxter is late, so we make a point of getting here early."

"How many children do you have here at this hour?" asked the father.

"It varies from week to week," replied the thirteen-year-old. "As you can see, right now we have only three, but I expect we'll have nine or ten and, every once in awhile we'll have a dozen or more."

"What happens if Mrs. Baxter doesn't get here?" asked the father as he looked at his watch and saw it was only four minutes before the scheduled beginning of the worship service.

"Oh, she'll be here," came the confident reply. "She's often late, but she almost always makes it. If she doesn't, we'll see if we can talk one of the mothers into helping."

While this conversation was taking place, four more children, ranging in age from five to forty months, had been left by parents who hurried off to worship.

"I think we'll take our baby to church with us this morning," declared the mother. Just as she turned to leave, a harried but friendly Mrs. Baxter arrived and exclaimed, "Oh, what a beautiful baby! We'll take good care of her for you. You're new here, aren't you?"

By the time Mrs. Baxter had finished her warm welcome, this couple were moving toward the stairs. "Thanks, we're just looking," explained the father. This couple carried their baby with them to the worship service where the child slept peacefully until the last hymn. When the baby began to cry, they quietly slipped out during the last verse of that hymn and went on their way to the parking lot. The following week they went to the next church on their shopping list as they continued their search for a new church home.

This incident illustrates the number-one criterion for evaluating the nursery. This is a simple, pragmatic test. Will the parents of today's firstborn children leave their baby in your nursery? If they are not willing to do that, your nursery flunks the critical test.

THE IMPORTANCE OF SYMBOLIC ACTS

In addition, this story also offers five other lessons. The most important is symbolic. What kind of reception, as you seek to expand the teaching ministry of your church, do you provide for first-time visitors?

Every church has only three alternatives open to it if the goal is to expand the teaching ministry. One is to increase the number of members who participate in it. A second is to attract people beyond the current membership. The third is a combination of the first two.

If the goal is to attract people beyond the current membership, the attainment of that goal requires not only attracting first-time visitors, but also encouraging them to return for a second visit. The availability of convenient parking, an abundance of redundant directional signs, the attractiveness of the nursery, and the reception accorded the first-time visitors symbolize the degree of commitment to that goal. Are the people willing to invest the extra effort required to encourage first-time visitors to return? The difference between a wish and a goal often is symbolized by a willingness to act.

WHAT YEAR IS IT?

A second lesson from this story is illustrated by the birth curve. In 1921, for the first time in American history, the number of live births exceeded three million. A gradual decline hit bottom in 1933 when only 2.3 million live births were recorded. A new record was set in 1943, when for only the second time in American history live births exceeded three million. After dropping below 3 million in both 1944 and 1945, a new record of 3.4 million was set in 1946. By 1956 that total exceeded 4.2 million and continued on that level through 1961 and 1962. A long gradual decline bottomed out in 1973–76 when, for the first time since 1945, the number of live births fell below 3.2 million annually. A long gradual increase followed and in 1989, for the first time since 1964, the number of live births exceeded 4 million.

Thus 1989–1994 represents the second largest baby boom in American history.[1] That means the quality of the nursery is an especially important factor during the late 1980s and early 1990s. (That also means that in 2003–2012, the quality of the ministry with teenagers will be an influential factor for churches seeking to expand their teaching program.)

WHEN DO THEY RETURN?

When do the people who dropped out of church as teenagers return? One answer is some never do. Another is when their faith journey brings them back. A third is in the months following the birth of their first child.

In contemporary terms this means many of the people born in the 1954–64 era (the first period in American history when live births exceeded four million year after year), who postponed marriage until their late twenties or early thirties, are marrying and having babies. That is a powerful factor behind this new baby boom of 1989–1994.

Thus the church seeking to reach these new parents, many of them in their thirties, will welcome them with an attractive, easy-to-find, and well-staffed nursery.

Inasmuch as many parents both provide and expect higher quality care for that first baby, the standard should be designed to satisfy the mother who brings her first child to your nursery. The mother who leaves her seventh child in your nursery probably has learned that babies are tough and have powerful survival instincts, and she may be less demanding.

WHO IS THE CLIENT?

The fourth of these five lessons concerns the client. Your number-one client is the mother of today's baby, not the elderly male trustee. She, not the elected leadership of your congregation, will make the crucial evaluation of the quality of your nursery.

A close second on that list of clients is the first-time visitor who is the parent of a baby who could be left in the nursery. If the nursery is unacceptable, that parent may continue to church-shop elsewhere next Sunday.

A third client consists of those parents who place their baby in the nursery while they participate in your weekday programming. Are they fully satisfied with your nursery?

WHAT ARE THE CRITERIA?

What are the criteria used to evaluate the nursery where you expect thirty-two-year-old mothers to leave that precious firstborn baby? While this is far from an exhaustive list, these two dozen questions offer a beginning.

1. How many parents refuse to leave their baby in your nursery? Can you ask them their reasons?

2. Who inspects your nursery? The trustees? The pastor? The Christian education committee? The custodian? Perhaps the best answer is a committee consisting of four mothers, each of whom has a firstborn child less than ten months old (they do not have to be members to be part of your inspection team), plus one or two militant and articulate leaders who are grandmothers.

3. Do you reserve offstreet parking spaces close to the entrance nearest the nursery for single-parent mothers?

4. Do you have a counter next to a wet sink where diapers can be changed and the caregiver's hands washed after changing that diaper?

5. Does the sign above that counter instruct the caregivers to disinfect the counter after use?

6. At peak hour of use, does the number of cribs exceed

the number of babies? In other words, do you expect more or fewer babies next week than were here this week?

7. Do you keep toddlers in the same room with babies in cribs?

8. Is the same trustworthy adult present every Sunday morning to welcome parents and to reinforce the parents' trust in the nursery?

9. Do teenagers come in during the week and scatter the toys around the room used for toddlers?

10. Are the toys in the toddlers' room appropriate for that age group?

11. How often are the work surfaces, trays, tables, and toys that children may put in their mouths washed and disinfected?

12. Is a tray or plastic container highly visible that is labeled, "Toys to be washed before use"?

13. What is your system for recording the names of parents and where they can be found in case of emergency?

14. What is your security system to guarantee that a stranger will not come in and walk off with someone's baby?

15. Do the caregivers arrive at least ten minutes before the first baby is expected to arrive, and are they expected to stay for at least five minutes after the normal time for the departure of the last baby?

16. Is the room clean? Moldy? Cluttered? Well-lighted?

17. Are there *no* small parts of toys that could be ingested or inhaled by very young children? Do the workers know the proper procedure if a child chokes?

18. Who washes the sheets, towels, and other linens? How often?

19. Is the nursery conveniently located in relationship to

the room most frequently used by mothers of young children in weekday programming?

20. What is the ratio of caregivers to babies? A minimum is one caregiver for every three children. The ideal is a one-to-one ratio.

21. Are the cribs fitted with clean sheets for every baby? After each service? Or are the sheets changed only once a week? Or once every month? Or every year? Or every time someone thinks of it? Or with the arrival of every new pastor?

22. Does the nursery include rocking chairs?

23. Are the babies, diaper bags, and bottles clearly marked with the infants' names?

THREE RELATED QUESTIONS

If the nursery is one part of a larger strategy for reaching and serving parents of young children, it may be useful to raise three other questions.

First, what is the quality of the women's restrooms? The comparison should not be with the restrooms before they were remodeled back in 1962 nor with the restrooms in the church down the street. The best comparison is with the restroom in that new shopping mall that young families patronize.

Second, do you have an attractive meeting room conveniently close to the nursery on the same floor that is an attractive place for a Sunday school class that includes parents of very young children? Can this room be used for weekday programming for parents who expect to bring their babies and leave them in the nursery? Or do you expect parents to participate in weekday evening programming far removed from where they will leave their babies?

Third, if the nursery is used by outside groups and organizations that meet in your building, what are the expectations of each group in regard to use of the nursery? How do members of outside groups know about these expectations?

These are few of the questions you may want to ask about the nursery in your church if you are seeking to reach this new generation of parents as a part of a larger strategy for expanding your teaching ministry.

CHAPTER FIFTEEN

Entry Points and Assimilation

For nearly two hundred years the Sunday school was widely perceived as the number-one educational arm of the Protestant churches on the North American continent. In recent decades this perspective has been expanded to conceptualize the Sunday school as only one of several components of an educational ministry. While no longer as popular as it was in the middle of this century, hundreds of churches have sought the services of a professionally trained director of Christian education. More recently the trend has been to broaden the focus and to strengthen the entire teaching ministry of the worshiping community. This broadened focus often begins with the sermon and includes a variety of teaching ministries, ranging from a Saturday morning men's Bible class to the weekday pre-kindergarten nursery school to classes on parenting to a systematic two- or three-year intensive study of the Holy Scriptures to the forty-five-week orientation class for prospective new members to a two- or three-year confirmation schedule for youth. From this perspective the Sunday school has moved over in a growing number of congregations to become only one of several components of a comprehensive teaching ministry.

A review of the experiences of scores of congregations that have followed this path raises four fascinating questions.

WHAT IF IT WORKS?

The first is one that often arises when something new and different is undertaken. What if it works? If the new idea proves to be a complete failure, very little changes. Life goes on as before. The big risk is that the new idea will be implemented and turn out to be a success story! This often results in change, discontinuity, and other disruptive experiences.

One example is when the new minister comes to serve a congregation that has gradually shrunk from an average worship attendance of 185 to 175 over the previous decade. The new minister comes and serves for nine years during which time the worship attendance drops to an average of 160 annually. That gradual attrition rarely is perceived as disruptive. The next pastor arrives, and seven years later the average worship attendance has nearly tripled to 425. This may be accompanied by such changes as the decision to construct a large addition to the building, adding a second full-time ordained minister to the staff, quadrupling the budget, and radically changing the Sunday morning schedule. Nearly everyone wanted to see their church change from growing older and smaller to growing younger and larger, but many were upset with some of the consequences of numerical growth.

A parallel often appears when the educational ministry oriented to the members is revised to become a teaching ministry designed for both members and seekers, searchers, and pilgrims who are on a religious quest. When that happens, the teaching ministry often becomes the biggest single entry point for potential future new members. As more and more new people are attracted by this teaching ministry, some of the oldtimers may question whether "the tail is now wagging the dog." These reservations about what has happened often are reinforced by the fact that the new and younger members bring a different value system than the one that guides the lives of the older longtime members. The most disruptive, of course, is when that new generation brings new and strange preferences for the music to be used in corporate worship.

WILL STRANGERS BE WELCOMED?

This leads to that second question. Do you want the teaching ministry to become an attractive entry point for newcomers to your church? For some readers the answer may be an immediate, "Of course! Why not?" For the leaders in many other churches, however, the urgent agenda item when the discussion turns to expanding the teaching ministry is, "How can we get more of our present members to participate in our educational program? We're not especially interested in reaching more people. Our top priority is doing a better job with the people we already count as members. We're already as big as we should be."

For most congregations that simple distinction between "serving our own people" and "reaching out to others" is more complex than it first appears. The most common reason why members do not participate in the teaching ministry of their own church is that they have decided it is irrelevant to their religious journey or boring or dull or hypocritical or designed for someone else. If that congregation decides to redesign the teaching ministry to make it attractive, meaningful, relevant, and responsive to the religious needs of the members, it probably also will be attractive to the searchers, sojourners, seekers, pilgrims, and others on a religious quest. Building a better mousetrap can cause people to beat a path to your door. Likewise, unless it is well concealed, redesigning the teaching ministry of your congregation to meet the religious needs of people can result in non-members coming to share in that feast.

Do you want that to happen? If you do, will you aggressively invite non-members to come? If you do, and if they do come, are you prepared to deal with the consequences of success? What if it works? What other changes will result? Do you really want to make the teaching ministry an attractive entry point for potential new members?

One example of this is the newly arrived pastor who preaches motivational and memorable sermons that challenge listeners to examine their personal belief system, how they live out their faith, and also how the gospel of Jesus Christ speaks to their personal needs. That in itself, however, while commendable, is not the key to attracting new members. The key is in the range of study groups, classes, and other opportunities that the congregation offers those listeners to pursue the questions raised in that sermon. This combination of a sermonic challenge combined with a programmatic response is a critical component of the teaching ministry designed to reach and serve the generations born after 1955.

If you decide you do want to use your teaching ministry to reach people not actively involved in the life of any worshiping community, and if you are prepared to pay the price of success, where do you begin?

SIX BEGINNING POINTS

That is the third of these four questions, and it does not have a simple answer that fits all. In one sense this entire book was designed to answer that question. To be more precise, however, a half dozen alternatives will illustrate a few of the possibilities.

If the goal is to reach the generations of adults born after 1940, one alternative is to begin with making the corporate worship experience a significant learning opportunity. This often includes (a) a highly sophisticated emphasis on visual communications, (b) drama, (c) a memorable reading of the Scripture lessons for the day, (d) a single central theme for that worship experience that is reinforced repeatedly, and (e) a carefully designed and memorable sermon that may be as long as thirty-five to sixty minutes. When people leave, they rejoice that they came for many reasons. One is that they left knowing more about the Christian faith than they knew when they came. More important, they leave convinced that that particular sermon was prepared to respond to the questions they carried in their hearts and their heads when they walked in that morning. They also leave absolutely convinced they know what this preacher believes. For some, they leave knowing what the next step is for them in their faith journey. Most leave convinced they will be spiritually nourished if they return the following Sunday. At least a few leave feeling grateful that they now can articulate what they thought they believed, but had never before been able to put into words. No one leaves feeling this was a waste of time but at least they have fulfilled their religious obligation for the week. All leave feeling better about their faith than they did when they walked in that morning.

An alternative approach for reaching the same generations is an extensive teaching ministry for adults carried on from Monday through Saturday with study groups meeting both daytime and in the evening.

If the goal is to reach upwardly mobile parents (both black and white as well as Hispanic and Asian) who have strong ambitions for their children, the Christian day school may be the best beginning point. This is best conceptualized as the centerpiece of a comprehensive package of ministries for families with young children.

If the goal is to reach young never-married adults and the formerly married, the beginning point may be a series of mutual support groups. One can be a response to the adult children of an alcoholic parent. Another could be for those adults who carry the scars from wounds received when, as teenagers, they became the victims of divorced parents. A third could be for those seeking to improve their skills in interpersonal relationships. In each, the curriculum places what has been learned about that particular need within the larger context of the teachings of the Christian faith.

If the goal is to reach parents of young children, both couples and single parents, this may be accomplished through the Sunday school and a range of continuing adult classes.

If the goal is to reach empty nest couples and mature adults living alone, one possibility is to invite them to help pioneer a new adult class in the Sunday school that eventually resembles the one described in the opening pages of the second chapter.

Overlapping all of these and other beginning points is an ancient axiom that needs to be emphasized. That axiom is "New groups for new people." If you are serious about the teaching ministry offering a series of attractive entry points for future new members, plan on creating new groups for new people. Do not expect everyone to be eager to join long-established classes!

THE FOURTH QUESTION

The last of the four questions to be discussed here reflects that threatening first question. What if it works? What if we do decide to make the teaching ministry our number-one entry point for future new members, and it works? What happens next? One need is to be prepared for other changes. Another is to examine the present system for the assimilation of new members.[1] A safe assumption is that no one system will work for everyone. What are the redundant or backup systems?

A common example is that the adult Sunday school described early in the first chapter can be highly effective in assimilating newcomers into that class, but many will continue to see themselves as outsiders in their relationship to the entire congregation.

Teaching in the Sunday school, working in the Vacation Bible School, serving on the Christian education committee, or volunteering as a counselor on field trips can help to facilitate the assimilation of parents who have children enrolled in the weekday teaching ministry.

Likewise the Surrogate Grandfathers' Club that is the combination blocking back-angel-patron-repairer of toys and support group for the weekday nursery school can be one channel for helping the men in that class of mature adults gain a sense of belonging to the larger fellowship.

The critical issue here, however, is not how, but if. If you do not conceptualize your teaching ministry as one component of a larger system for the assimilation of newcomers, it probably will be less than adequately effective. The key is for every leader, both volunteer and paid, to accept the premise that your teaching ministry also can be a major contributor to the assimilation of newcomers. Is that an acceptable goal for you and your colleagues?

NOTES

2. WHAT ARE YOUR CRITERIA?

1. Ray Oldenburg, *The Great Good Place* (New York: Paragon House, 1989).
2. A superb study of Christian education in six American Protestant denominations was published in early 1990. Among other contributions, this study offers criteria for the evaluation of Christian education. The summary report, *Effective Christian Education: A National Study of Protestant Congregations—A summary report on faith, loyalty and congregational life*, was written by Peter L. Benson and Carolyn H. Eklin. This volume, plus reports on the findings for each of the six participating denominations, can be purchased from Search Institute, Suite 525, 122 W. Franklin Ave., Minneapolis, MN 55404.

3. A CRITICAL VARIABLE

1. H. Leon McBeth, *Celebrating Heritage & Hope* (Nashville: Broadman Press, 1990).
2. For further suggestions see Robert L. Browning, ed., *The Pastor as Religious Educator* (Birmingham, Ala.: Religious Education Press, 1989).
3. Neil Postman, *Amusing Ourselves to Death* (New York: Penguin Press, 1986).

4. WHAT IS THE INSTITUTIONAL CONTEXT?

1. Benson and Eklin, *Effective Christian Education*, p. 17.
2. Examples of other models of congregational life are

described in Lyle E. Schaller, *Choices for Churches* (Nashville: Abingdon Press, 1990), pp. 19-56.

5. FIFTEEN BENCHMARKS

1. Benson and Eklin, *Effective Christian Education*, p. 9.
2. For a longer discussion on canceling the summer slump, see Lyle E. Schaller, *44 Ways to Increase Church Attendance* (Nashville: Abingdon Press, 1988), pp. 71-74.
3. While the quality of the analysis leaves much to be desired, the recent rapid growth and the variety of mutual support groups is reviewed in "Unite and Conquer," *Newsweek*, February 5, 1990, pp. 50-55.

6. WHO IS THE CLIENT?

1. Anne M. Boylan, *Sunday School: The Formation of an American Institution* (New Haven: Yale University Press, 1988), p. 7.

7. BUILDING IN CONTINUITY

1. Alvin Toffler, *Future Shock* (New York: Random House, 1970), pp. 324-37.
2. The value of long-term teacher-pupil relationships in the Sunday school was affirmed in an article published in 1824 when it was recommended that the practice of rotating teaching staffs be abandoned in favor of year-long assignments to one class. Boylan, *Sunday School*, p. 135.

8. FUNCTION, THEME, OR ORGANIZATION?

1. Schaller, *Choices for Churches*, pp. 29-32, and Boylan, *Sunday School*, pp. 1-5, 60-100. The denominational challenges to this interdenominational movement are discussed by Boyland, pp. 77-84.
2. A more extensive discussion of the characteristics of a move-

ment can be found in Lyle E. Schaller, *Getting Things Done* (Nashville: Abingdon Press, 1986), chap. 2.

9. FIFTEEN QUESTIONS FOR THE SUNDAY SCHOOL

1. For a provocative description of the place of the sermon in earlier days see Postman, *Amusing Ourselves to Death*, pp. 41-63.

2. Boylan, *Sunday School*, p. 3.

3. An excellent book on this subject is Dick Murray, *Strengthening the Adult Sunday School Class* (Nashville: Abingdon Press, 1981).

4. Oldenburg, *The Great Good Place*.

5. Benson and Eklin, *Effective Christian Education*.

6. Every resource center should consider subscribing to the *Harvard Educational Newsletter* (79 Garden Street, Cambridge, MA 02138-1423) and other periodicals. Another useful periodical is *Children Today*, published by the Office of Human Development Services in the United States Department of Health and Human Services. One designed specifically for teachers is *Teacher in the Church Today* (Cokesbury, P. O. Box 801, Nashville, TN 37202). Two excellent journals are *Child Development*, published by the University of Chicago Press and *Childhood Education*, published by the Association for Childhood Education International, Suite 200, 11141 Georgia Avenue, Wheaton, MD 20902. A newsletter that summarizes research on the family is *The Family in America*, 934 North Main Street, Rockford, IL 61103-7061. The cost of these subscriptions usually can be covered by one special offering annually.

Another possibility is to watch for relevant articles in newspapers, magazines, and journals and post these on the wall of the resource room. An excellent example of this is Daniel Coleman, "Child's Skills at Play Crucial to Success, New Studies Find," *New York Times*, October 3, 1990.

7. See Boylan, *Sunday School*, and Schaller, *Getting Things Done*, chaps. 2 and 7 for a more extended discussion of movements and rallying points.

8. For a superb introduction to the research on American youth

see Francis A. J. Ianni, *The Search for Structure: A Report on American Youth Today* (New York: The Free Press, 1989).

9. The SEARCH research referred to earlier suggests that this should be at the top of the priority list for your teaching ministry. Benson and Eklin, *Effective Christian Education*.

10. Ibid.

11. A provocative essay on the future of the Sunday school has been written by Tim Stafford, "This Little Light of Mine," *Christianity Today*, October 8, 1990, pp. 29-32.

10. WHY HAVE ADULT CLASSES?

1. For more detailed suggestions on the role of the long-range planning committee, see Lyle E. Schaller, *Create Your Own Future!* (Nashville: Abingdon Press, 1991).

2. For a longer explanation of how various models of congregational life encourage or inhibit numerical growth, see Schaller, *Choices for Churches*, pp. 19-57.

3. For a more detailed description of the pastor's class, see Lyle E. Schaller, *The Senior Minister* (Nashville: Abingdon Press, 1988), pp. 146-48.

11. WHAT IS THE ROLE OF PARENTS?

1. An introduction to the Missouri program can be found in Susan Caminiti, "A Bigger Role for Parents," *Fortune*, special 1990 education issue, pp. 25-32.

13. WHERE ARE THE MEN?

1. Oldenburg, *The Great Good Place*.

2. Toffler, *Future Shock*, pp. 324-37.

3. Benson and Eklin, *Effective Christian Education*, pp. 16-18 and 45-64.

14. THE NURSERY

1. At this writing it is still too early to offer a definitive statement, but preliminary reports from the National Center for Health Statistics suggest a new record for the number of live births in one year in the United States may be set in 1992 or 1993.

15. ENTRY POINTS AND ASSIMILATION

1. See Lyle E. Schaller, *Assimilating New Members* (Nashville: Abingdon Press, 1978).